Table of Contents

Introduction

What Is Readers' Theater?

One good way to gain an understanding of readers' theater is to first get a clear picture of what it is *not*. Readers' theater is not a fully-staged production with sets, costumes, and dramatic action performed by actors who memorize lines from a script. Instead, a readers' theater performance is a dramatic reading, just as its name suggests. Readers are usually seated, reading from a script that is held in their hands or placed on a music stand in front of them. There may be minimal use of costumes or props, such as hats, a scepter or crown, or a simple backdrop to provide a suggestion of the setting and characters that the readers hope to bring to life for the audience during their dramatic reading.

Readers' theater offers all the enrichment of traditional theater productions, but without the logistical challenges that come with designing and building sets and creating costumes. Students are spared the stress of having to memorize lines, and can instead focus on developing a strong dramatic reading of the script.

How to Integrate *Readers' Theater* into Your Classroom

The *Readers' Theater* scripts may be used in a variety of settings for a range of educational purposes. Consider the following:

Language Arts blocks are ideal for incorporating *Readers' Theater* scripts, with their emphasis on reading aloud with expression. Many of the follow-up activities that accompany each script address key skills from the reading/language arts curriculum.

Content-Area Instruction can come alive when you use a *Readers' Theater* script to help explore social studies, science, or math concepts. Check the Table of Contents for the grade-level content-area connections in each script.

Integrated Thematic Teaching can continue throughout the day when you use *Readers' Theater* scripts to help you maintain your thematic focus across all areas of the curriculum, from language arts instruction through content-area lessons.

School Assemblies and Holiday Programs provide the perfect opportunity to showcase student performances. Consider presenting a *Readers' Theater* performance for Black History Month, Women's History Month, for parent evenings, or any other occasion when your students are invited to perform.

Teaching the *Readers' Theater* Units

The 15 units in this volume each include the following:

- A **teacher page** to help you plan instruction:

A short **summary** gives you an overview of each script's plot.

Use the **number of parts** to choose the number of readers to assign per role. Or, you may wish to create two or more casts for each production.

Background information provides facts that you may need to know about the subject treated in the script. It also guides you in activating students' prior knowledge or in building background about new or unfamiliar topics. This helps promote success for students as they approach each new script.

A **unit-level table of contents** gives you at-a-glance information on the script and the follow-up activities.

Vocabulary that may be new or unfamiliar to students is called out so that you can introduce it prior to reading the script.

Staging ideas may be included for some scripts. These optional ideas offer quick and easy suggestions to help both readers and their audience connect with the characters and setting of the play.

An **encore** feature for some scripts includes quick, optional ideas to extend learning related to the content of the script. Ideas range from retelling activities and related literature to ideas for other types of performances.

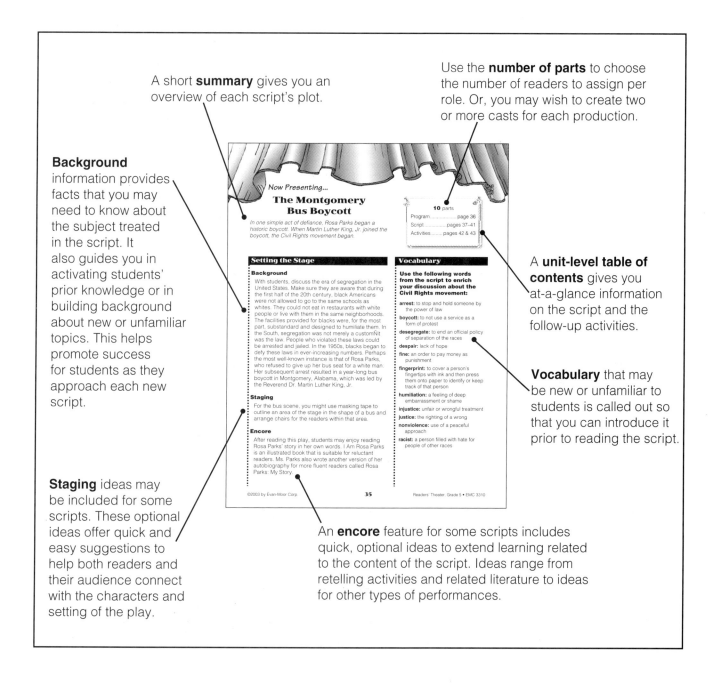

Now Presenting...

The Montgomery Bus Boycott

In one simple act of defiance, Rosa Parks began a historic boycott. When Martin Luther King, Jr. joined the boycott, the Civil Rights movement began.

10 parts

Program	page 36
Script	pages 37–41
Activities	pages 42 & 43

Setting the Stage

Background

With students, discuss the era of segregation in the United States. Make sure they are aware that during the first half of the 20th century, black Americans were not allowed to go to the same schools as whites. They could not eat in restaurants with white people or live with them in the same neighborhoods. The facilities provided for blacks were, for the most part, substandard and designed to humiliate them. In the South, segregation was not merely a custom—it was the law. People who violated these laws could be arrested and jailed. In the 1950s, blacks began to defy these laws in ever-increasing numbers. Perhaps the most well-known instance is that of Rosa Parks, who refused to give up her bus seat for a white man. Her subsequent arrest resulted in a year-long bus boycott in Montgomery, Alabama, which was led by the Reverend Dr. Martin Luther King, Jr.

Staging

For the bus scene, you might use masking tape to outline an area of the stage in the shape of a bus and arrange chairs for the readers within that area.

Encore

After reading this play, students may enjoy reading Rosa Parks' story in her own words. I Am Rosa Parks is an illustrated book that is suitable for reluctant readers. Ms. Parks also wrote another version of her autobiography for more fluent readers called Rosa Parks: My Story.

Vocabulary

Use the following words from the script to enrich your discussion about the Civil Rights movement:

arrest: to stop and hold someone by the power of law

boycott: to not use a service as a form of protest

desegregate: to end an official policy of separation of the races

despair: lack of hope

fine: an order to pay money as punishment

fingerprint: to cover a person's fingertips with ink and then press them onto paper to identify or keep track of that person

humiliation: a feeling of deep embarrassment or shame

injustice: unfair or wrongful treatment

justice: the righting of a wrong

nonviolence: use of a peaceful approach

racist: a person filled with hate for people of other races

©2003 by Evan-Moor Corp. 35 Readers' Theater, Grade 5 • EMC 3310

- A reproducible **program** page provides an introduction to the script and a list of characters. Use this page to list the names of students who will read each role, and distribute it to your audience to enhance the theater-going experience.

- The **script** is the heart of the *Readers' Theater* volume. This is the reproducible four- or five-page text that students will read during rehearsals and performances. You may wish to read the script aloud to students before assigning parts and beginning rehearsal readings. Once you have read through the script as a group, you may wish to assign students to work independently in small groups while you interact with other student groups.

- Two or three pages of follow-up **activities** may be assigned once students have completed a first reading of the script. Activities are designed to be completed independently, and may be conducted while you provide individualized or small-group instruction or hold a rehearsal with another group of students.

Meeting Individual Needs

Struggling readers may be partnered with one or more stronger readers who all read the same role together. This group support is often enough to allow struggling readers to participate fully in the activity. Struggling readers may also be able to independently read parts that have a repeating refrain or a simple rhyme pattern.

Students acquiring English may benefit from using the same approaches as for struggling readers. In addition, you may wish to create an audio recording of the script to provide English learners the opportunity to listen to fluent English pronunciation of the script as they follow along with the written text.

Accelerated learners may be challenged to transform *Readers' Theater* scripts into fully-staged productions by adding stage directions, planning props and sets, and even developing or expanding the existing dialog. You might also use such students as "directors," helping to manage small-group rehearsals for class *Readers' Theater* productions.

Evaluating Student Performance

Use the templates provided on pages 5 and 6 to help students plan and evaluate their performances. You may copy and distribute the templates just as they are, or use them to guide you in leading a class discussion about the criteria for evaluating *Readers' Theater* performances. Students may also develop their own iconography (e.g., one or two thumbs up, thumbs down, 1 to 5 stars, etc.) to rate their own performances and those of their classmates. Encourage students to be thoughtful in providing feedback, stressing the importance of sharing ways to improve, as well as highlighting successful aspects of the performance. You may wish to conduct performance reviews during the rehearsal stage in order to give students an opportunity to incorporate suggestions for improvement. You may also wish to compare those comments to feedback following the final performance. Use the template on page 7 to conduct your own assessment of students' acquisition of language arts skills during *Readers' Theater* activities.

Pre-performance Checklist

Name _____

1. Did you listen to or participate in a first reading of the script?
   ☐ **Yes**
   ☐ **No** – Watch a group rehearsal if hearing the script aloud is helpful for you.

2. Did you highlight all your lines in the script?
   ☐ **Yes**
   ☐ **No** – Use a highlighting pen to go over all your lines.

3. Did you mark places where you must pause between lines?
   ☐ **Yes**
   ☐ **No** – Use a mark like this: / /

4. Have you collected any materials or props that you will use?
   ☐ **Yes**
   ☐ **No** – Ask your teacher or other cast members for ideas if you need help.

5. Have you chosen and practiced any movements, faces, or speaking styles you will use?
   ☐ **Yes**
   ☐ **No** – Ask your teacher or other cast members for ideas if you need help.

6. Have you practiced reading your lines with expression?
   ☐ **Yes**
   ☐ **No** – Try out your ideas with a partner or another cast member.

7. Have you participated in a rehearsal and gotten performance feedback?
   ☐ **Yes**
   ☐ **No** – Have a reviewer focus on your participation in the play. After you get feedback, find ways to make changes to improve your performance.

Performance Review Template

Date: _____ Title of play: _____

☐ Rehearsal
☐ Performance

1. I am reviewing
   ☐ one reader   Name: _____   Role: _____
   ☐ the entire performance

2. I could see the reader(s).
   ☐ Yes
   ☐ Needs improvement   Name(s): _____

3. I could hear the reader(s).
   ☐ Yes
   ☐ Needs to speak more loudly   Name(s): _____

4. I could understand the reader(s).
   ☐ Yes
   ☐ Needs to speak more clearly   Name(s): _____

5. The reader(s) used good expression.
   ☐ Yes
   ☐ Needs to improve   Name(s): _____

6. The use of gestures was
   ☐ just right
   ☐ not enough; use more
   ☐ too much; use fewer   Name(s): _____

7. Some things that were done well:

   _____

   _____

8. Some things that could be done better, and some ideas for improving them:

   _____

   _____

Assessing Oral Presentations

As you observe students during rehearsals or performances, focus on the following areas in assessing individual students.

Date: _____

Title of play: _____

☐ Rehearsal

☐ Performance

Name: _____   Role: _____

1. Student speaks clearly.	☐ Yes	☐ Needs improvement
2. Student speaks at appropriate pace.	☐ Yes	☐ Needs improvement
3. Student speaks fluently, using appropriate intonation, expression, and emphasis.	☐ Yes	☐ Needs improvement
4. Student enlivens reading with gestures and facial expressions.	☐ Yes	☐ Needs improvement
5. Student prepared and used appropriate props.	☐ Yes	☐ Not applicable
6. Student participated actively in rehearsals.	☐ Yes	☐ Needs improvement
7. Student contributed appropriately to this production.	☐ Yes	☐ Needs improvement

Other comments: _____

_____

_____

_____

_____

Now Presenting...

Demeter and Persephone

The story of Demeter and her daughter Persephone is a popular Greek myth. It explains how the seasons correspond to the tearful separation and joyful reunion of mother and daughter.

Setting the Stage

Background

Ask students what they know about Greek mythology. You might have them summarize some of these stories or tell about the characters. Point out that the Greek gods lived in a heavenly palace on Mount Olympus. The Greek universe was further divided into two other realms: the world of mortals; and the Underworld, which was ruled by Hades. The gods and mortals in this play pass through all three realms of the Greek universe. This is a nature myth, which explains how the seasons came to be.

Staging

Students may create crowns for the gods Zeus and Demeter. They may also use a cane to represent the shepherd's staff. The character of Hades may wear a dark robe. In contrast, Persephone may wear a light-colored robe or scarf around her shoulders.

Encore

Students will surely be curious to learn more about Greek mythology after reading this play. The following gods and other characters are all featured in Greek nature myths: Prometheus, Pandora, Phaethon, Orpheus, Narcissus, Echo, Eros, Psyche, and Arion. Assign groups to find out about one or two characters, and have them share the corresponding myth with the class.

Vocabulary

Introduce and discuss the following words before reading the script:

abode: the place where one lives

bestow: to formally give something to somebody as a gift

eavesdrop: to listen to a conversation in secret

mortal: a human being

regret: to wish a past action had not happened

traipse: to walk about in an absent-minded, lighthearted way

Now Presenting...

Demeter and Persephone

In grief over her missing daughter, the goddess Demeter takes back all the gifts she has given to the earth.

Characters

Narrator .... _____

Demeter .... _____
(goddess of growing things)

Persephone .... _____
(daughter of Demeter)

Shepherd .... _____

Hades .... _____
(god of the Underworld)

Zeus .... _____
(king of the gods)

Hermes .... _____
(messenger of the gods)

     Readers' Theater, Grade 5 • EMC 3310

Demeter and Persephone

········· Characters ·········

Narrator Hades
Demeter Zeus
Persephone Hermes
Shepherd

Narrator: In a time before time, the world was ruled by the gods of Mount Olympus. Demeter was the goddess of green and growing things. She bestowed her gifts on the earth all year 'round. Demeter dearly loved her daughter Persephone and allowed her to play amidst the mortals on Earth. One day, Persephone was traipsing through a meadow tended by a shepherd.

Shepherd: Good morning, Persephone. What good fortune brings you here today?

Persephone: I'm gathering flowers for my dear mother. Have you seen any nearby?

Shepherd: If it's flowers you're looking for, go to the edge of the meadow. I saw a patch of flowers there this morning.

Persephone: Thank you, kind shepherd.

Narrator: Persephone had no idea that somebody was eavesdropping on her conversation with the shepherd. That somebody was Hades, lord of the Underworld. As Hades listened to Persephone, he was devising an unthinkable scheme.

Hades: Dearest Persephone, how sweet and innocent you are. In a moment, you will fall into my trap. And then you will be mine forever and ever.

Narrator: At that moment, Persephone noticed a small flower growing all by itself. It was the loveliest flower she had ever seen. When she bent down to pick it up, a deep crack split open in the earth and swallowed her up. Persephone fell for miles and miles until she landed in the lap of the Underworld.

Persephone: *(dazed)* Where am I? And who in the world are you?

Hades: I am none other than Hades, and this is my kingdom. Welcome to my abode.

Persephone: What do you want with me?

Hades: I have brought you here to be my wife. Together, we will rule as king and queen.

Persephone: No! I must return to my mother! Let me go at once!

Hades: You can protest all you want, but you will waste your breath. Nobody can hear your cries from here, not even your mother.

Persephone: You'll regret this. The almighty Zeus will surely hear of your wrongdoing. When he does, you will have to pay serious consequences.

Hades: Zeus has no power over me. It's better if you simply accept your destiny, Persephone. You'll get used to it over time.

Persephone: Never!

Narrator: At sunset, Demeter began to get worried about Persephone. She searched through all the fields and meadows, calling out her name. Finally, she came upon the shepherd who had seen Persephone earlier that day.

Demeter: *(loudly)* Persephone! Where are you? . . . *(to shepherd)* Have you seen my daughter?

Shepherd: Persephone is your daughter? Then you are the goddess Demeter! How may I serve you?

Demeter: Please, good shepherd, tell me if you have seen my daughter Persephone.

Shepherd: Yes I have, O Mighty One. She was here this morning.

Demeter: What happened to her? Tell me quickly!

Shepherd: Hades kidnapped her. She is now his prisoner in the Underworld.

Demeter: Noooo! My one and only daughter! Gone forever!

Narrator: Demeter was crazy with grief. She went up to Mount Olympus, taking with her all the gifts she had bestowed upon the earth. Sunlight dwindled and the days grew shorter and colder. The trees were bare; flowers froze and died. People of the world raised their voices to the goddess, begging her to return. Finally, the almighty Zeus heard their pleas from his throne in heaven.

Zeus: What's that I hear?

Hermes: It is the sound of sadness and grief. Demeter mourns her missing daughter, Persephone. In her grief, she has taken away nature's bounty. The people cry out for her return.

Zeus: You say that Persephone is missing?

Hermes: She disappeared without a trace.

Zeus: Go find her, Hermes. Do not come back until you do. Anyone who has harmed her will face the wrath of Zeus.

Narrator: Hermes flew down to Earth in the blink of an eye. After many days without sleep or rest, he at last found the shepherd who had last seen Persephone.

Hermes: You say she was kidnapped by Hades?

Shepherd: I swear by all the gods on Mount Olympus.

Hermes: Show me where she disappeared.

Narrator: The kind old shepherd guided Hermes to the crack in the meadow. In a flash, Hermes had slipped into the earth, following the passageway all the way to the heart of the Underworld. There was Hades, seated on his throne. Next to him was Persephone.

Persephone: Hermes, at last you've found me! Where is my mother?

Hermes: Waiting for your return. Come, I will take you from this place and reunite you with your beloved mother.

Hades: Not so fast! Persephone is now queen of the Underworld. This is where she belongs.

Hermes: Do not hold her against her will, Hades. Heed my words, or you will face the wrath of Zeus.

Hades: But I am *not* holding her against her will. She is here of her own free choosing.

Hermes: Is this true, Persephone?

Persephone: Yes, dear Hermes. Now that I have been here for almost a year, I have grown fond of Hades. I know it is my destiny to live here forever, yet I yearn to see my mother.

Hades: I have grown fond of you too, Persephone. To please you, I shall send you to see your grieving mother and take away her pain. Stay with her for a spell of time, then come back. Tell Demeter that I shall send you to visit her at the same time every year.

Persephone: My lord, you are generous and kind. I will go as you say, and come back after six moons. Take my hand, Hermes, and lead the way.

Narrator: Demeter was overjoyed to see her daughter once again. As mother and daughter swayed together in their love for each other, the fields overflowed with nature's bounty. When the time came for Persephone to leave, Demeter withdrew her gifts once again in grief. And so it is every year. To this day, the changing seasons tell the story of Demeter's grief and her joyful reunion with her beloved daughter, Persephone.

In Other Words

Write the number of each word from the myth next to its synonym.

1. bestow	_____ abundance
2. traipse	_____ desire
3. fortune	_____ provide
4. eavesdrop	_____ notice
5. abode	_____ overhear
6. dwindle	_____ wander
7. mourn	_____ home
8. wrath	_____ decrease
9. yearn	_____ luck
10. bounty	_____ fury
11. generous	_____ giving
12. heed	_____ grieve

Choose four words from the list above. Use each in a sentence.

1. _____

2. _____

3. _____

4. _____

Name _____

The Three Worlds of
Ancient Greece

The ancient Greeks believed the world was divided into three realms: the Underworld, the world of humans, and Mount Olympus. Draw to show what you think each of these realms might look like.

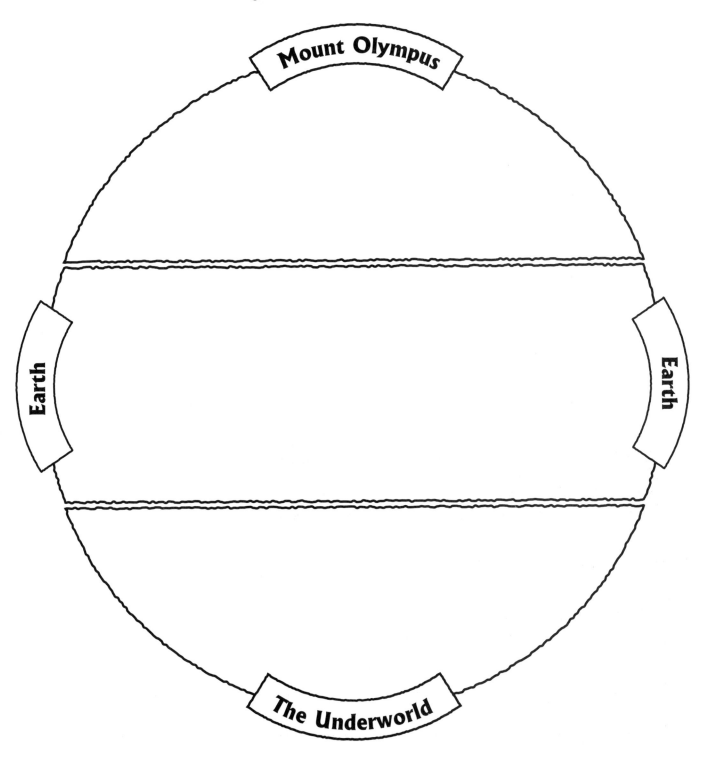

Greek Roots

Many English words are based on Greek roots. Study the root words in the table. Use these word parts to create a word for each definition below. Use a dictionary to check your work.

astro = star	**auto** = self	**bio** = life
graph/graphy = written	**ology** = the study of	**naut** = sailor
nomy = the study of	**phono** = sound	**photo** = light
psycho = mind	**tele** = from a distance	

1. _____ = a traveler in space

2. _____ = the study of outer space

3. _____ = the story of one's own life

4. _____ = a person's signature

5. _____ = the story of a person's life

6. _____ = the study of life

7. _____ = an instrument used to play a vinyl disk

8. _____ = an image taken by a camera

9. _____ = the study of the mind

10. _____ = an instrument that allows two people
in different places to converse

Now Presenting...

SOS *Titanic*

When the Titanic starts to sink, the fight for survival begins. This play is about the rescue mission following the horrors of the Titanic shipwreck.

7 parts

Setting the Stage

Background

Tell students that this play is based on the true story of the *Titanic,* a luxury liner that sank in the Atlantic Ocean in 1912. The *Titanic* began its maiden voyage from the port of Southampton, in England, on April 10. There were bad omens right from the beginning. Just after its launch, for example, the *Titanic* nearly crashed into another ship. After stopping at ports in France and Ireland, it made its way toward New York City. On the night of April 14, other ships sent the *Titanic* warnings about ice, but these warnings were ignored. There was a shortage of binoculars on board, so the lookouts could only peer into the darkness ahead. Shortly before midnight, the *Titanic* rammed into an iceberg. The *Carpathia* received an SOS signal from the *Titanic,* and headed for the site full steam ahead. It was nearly 60 miles away, however, and time was of the essence. In the end, nearly two-thirds of the *Titanic's* crew and passengers perished at sea.

Staging

Students may use caps and whistles as props for the crew of the *Titanic* and the *Carpathia.*

Encore

Students may enjoy watching movie versions of this historical disaster, including the black-and-white classic *A Night to Remember.*

Vocabulary

Introduce and discuss the following words before reading the script. Tell students that the following terms are all related to travel at sea. Have students look up the definitions and then use these words in sentences:

bow: the front section of a boat or ship

disembark: to get off a boat or ship

knots: a rate of speed equal to about 1.5 miles per hour

latitude: the distance north or south of the equator, measured in degrees

longitude: the distance east or west of the prime meridian, measured in degrees

maiden: first; untested

Morse code: a code consisting of short and long radio signals

SOS: a distress signal used internationally, especially by ships

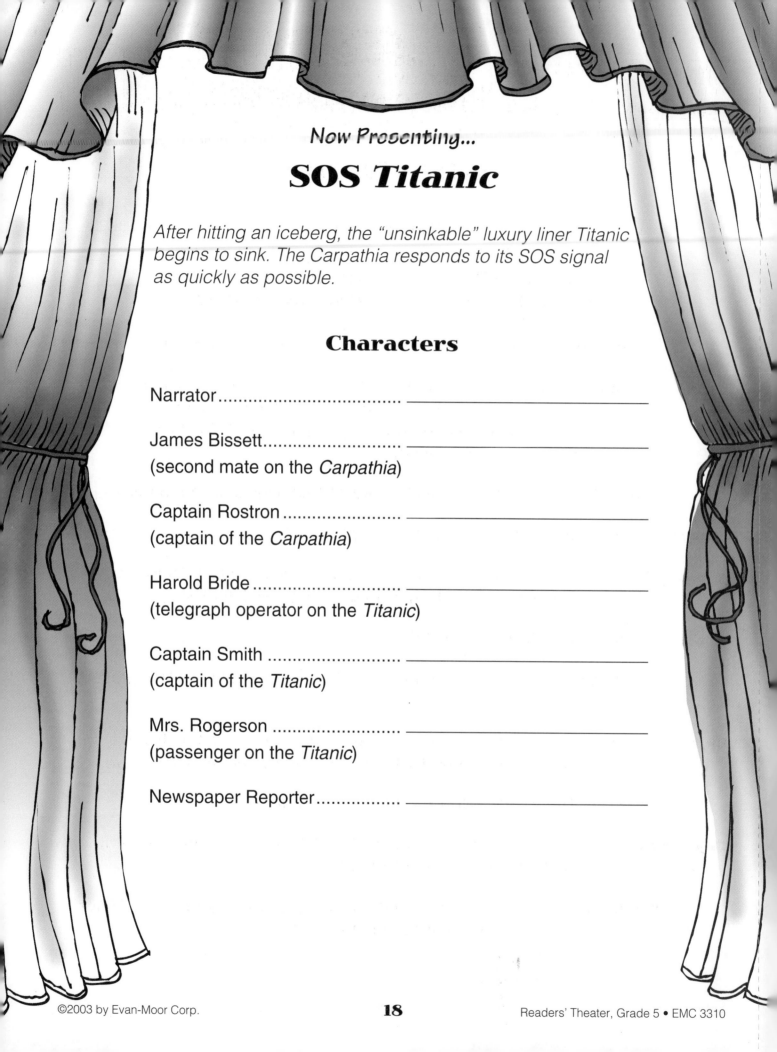

Now Presenting...

SOS Titanic

After hitting an iceberg, the "unsinkable" luxury liner Titanic begins to sink. The Carpathia responds to its SOS signal as quickly as possible.

Characters

Narrator.................................... _____

James Bissett............................ _____
(second mate on the *Carpathia*)

Captain Rostron .... _____
(captain of the *Carpathia*)

Harold Bride .... _____
(telegraph operator on the *Titanic*)

Captain Smith .... _____
(captain of the *Titanic*)

Mrs. Rogerson .... _____
(passenger on the *Titanic*)

Newspaper Reporter............... _____

SOS *Titanic*

····················· **Characters** ·····················

Narrator   Captain Smith
James Bissett   Mrs. Rogerson
Captain Rostron   Newspaper Reporter
Harold Bride

Narrator: Shortly after midnight on April 15, 1912, the ocean liner *Carpathia* received a distress signal. James Bissett, the second mate on the *Carpathia,* rushed to tell Captain Rostron the terrible news.

Bissett: Captain, we've just received an SOS signal. It's from the *Titanic.*

Captain Rostron: What exactly does the message say?

Bissett: It said they struck an iceberg and that the ship is badly damaged. The *Titanic* is sinking, Captain. They need our help.

Captain Rostron: What's their location?

Bissett: The latitude is 41 degrees north. The longitude is 50 degrees west.

Captain Rostron: That's almost 58 miles away. This old ship can't go faster than 16 knots per hour. It'll take us almost five hours to get there.

Bissett: The *Titanic* will surely be gone by then.

Captain Rostron: Then don't waste any time! Get the whole crew on deck, and push the engines to full speed!

Narrator: Meanwhile, on the *Titanic,* passengers were gathering on deck to receive instructions from the captain.

Captain Smith: Ladies and gentleman, please don't be alarmed. Panic will only make things worse. Kindly put on your safety vests and prepare to board the lifeboats. Women and children will go first. After that, the men may disembark.

Mrs. Rogerson: The *Titanic* can't possibly sink. After all, she was built to be unsinkable. And this is her maiden voyage. Who ever heard of a ship sinking its first time out? I think I'll just stay here.

Captain Smith: Please try to cooperate, Mrs. Rogerson.

Mrs. Rogerson: But I don't know the first thing about handling a lifeboat.

Captain Smith: A member of our crew will be on each of the lifeboats. Harold Bride, our telegraph operator, will be on your boat. You're in good hands.

Bride: *(to Mrs. Rogerson)* Here, let me help you get into the lifeboat. I'll hold your hand while you step onto the rope ladder.

Mrs. Rogerson: I don't like this one bit, but I'll cooperate, as you say.

Narrator: Mrs. Rogerson boarded the lifeboat with Harold Bride and six other passengers. Most of the lifeboats were only half full, as many people refused to accept the gravity of their situation. Then, at about half past two in the morning, there was a long, groaning sound as the *Titanic* began to tilt and sink into the ocean. With hundreds of passengers still aboard, panic broke out on the ship.

Captain Smith: *(in the distance)* Every man for himself!

Mrs. Rogerson: What's that? What is going on?

Bride: The unbelievable has happened. The *Titanic* is sinking.

Mrs. Rogerson: Oh, my word! The ship is tilting straight out of the water! I wouldn't believe it if I weren't seeing it with my own eyes. Thank goodness Captain Smith persuaded me to board the lifeboat.

Bride: The lights just went out. The power on board must have been cut. Now I can't see a thing. It's so quiet. It's *too* quiet.

Mrs. Rogerson: Oh, those poor, foolish people! And to think I might still have been onboard along with the rest of them! Perhaps they'll be able to swim over to the lifeboats. Surely there is room for more people.

Bride: I don't see how they can last more than a minute or two in this water. It's freezing cold.

Mrs. Rogerson: I can barely stand the cold myself. When will help come? How long will we have to wait out here in the freezing cold? My hands have grown numb and my face is freezing.

Bride: Rub your hands together and blow on them. Let's sit back to back and hold this blanket around our shoulders to keep warm. Help is on the way. I'm sure of that, because I sent the SOS signal myself.

Narrator: The lifeboat passengers shivered for several hours as they waited. When the sun rose, the *Titanic* was nowhere to be seen. In its place was the *Carpathia.*

Captain Rostron: Ready at the bow! Here comes the first lifeboat.

Mrs. Rogerson: *(boarding the ship)* Oh, thank goodness you've arrived. I wasn't sure how much longer I could take the cold. Oh, my hands— I can't feel my hands at all!

Captain Rostron: Right this way, ma'am. The ship's doctor is ready to help. We've got hot cocoa and warm blankets waiting for you in the hold. *(to Bissett)* James, help get her over to the first aid area, and be gentle. She's a bit unsteady. Then report back to help someone else. They just keep on coming. Here's another one. Who are you?

Bride: *(in a raspy voice)* My name's Bride. Harold Bride.

Captain Rostron: You're the one who sent the SOS signal. If it weren't for you, the disaster would have been even worse. Come onboard.

Bride: I don't think I can walk. My feet are frozen.

Captain Rostron: Don't worry. The medical crew is ready to treat you for frostbite. Here, let me help you. Easy does it.

Narrator: Later that day, Captain Rostron held a service for the victims of the *Titanic* disaster on the very spot where they had gone down with the ship. Then the *Carpathia* made its way to New York City. When the ship docked, thousands of people were anxiously waiting at the pier. The *Titanic* disaster was front-page news around the world. A reporter interviewed the crew and passengers as they disembarked.

Reporter: Captain, how in the world did something like this happen?

Captain Rostron: There was a whole series of mistakes. The *Titanic* was warned about icebergs, but Captain Smith ignored the warnings. To top it off, the crew of the *Titanic* wasn't prepared to deal with the emergency.

Reporter: *(to Mrs. Rogerson)* Would you agree with that, ma'am?

Mrs. Rogerson: I don't think anybody realized what was happening until it was too late. Maybe Captain Smith knew that the ship was going to sink, but he was very calm about it. I think he didn't want to frighten the passengers.

Reporter: Did you see the ship sinking?

Mrs. Rogerson: Yes, it tilted out of the water at a steep angle, and then it just started to sink. Some said that the ship actually snapped in half, but it's hard to say what happened. It was so dark.

Reporter: Thank you, ma'am. *(to Bride)* Sir, I hear that you're the one who sent the SOS signal.

Bride: That I am.

Reporter: Mr. Bride, did you know that this is the very first instance of a ship sending an SOS signal by Morse code?

Bride: Unfortunately, many things happened last night that have never happened before. If we learn some important lessons from this disaster, perhaps such a tragedy will never happen again.

Narrator: The sinking of the *Titanic* was a horrible disaster. Of the 2,224 people on board, there were only 705 survivors. Because of this catastrophe, many safety regulations are now in place to make sure an accident like this never happens again.

SOS

Mr. Bride sent an SOS message by Morse code. On paper, the Morse code is made up of dots and dashes. A dot represents a very short signal, and a dash is three times longer.

Letter	Morse		Letter	Morse		Letter	Morse
A	• –		J	• – – –		S	• • •
B	– • • •		K	– • –		T	–
C	– • – •		L	• – • •		U	• • –
D	– • •		M	– –		V	• • • –
E	•		N	– •		W	• – –
F	• • – •		O	– – –		X	– • • –
G	– – •		P	• – – •		Y	– • – –
H	• • • •		Q	– – • –		Z	– – • •
I	• •		R	• – •			

Decode this message in Morse code. Write the corresponding letter under each Morse signal.

• • •   • –   • • • –   •   –   • • • •   •

_____ _____ _____ _____ _____ _____

–   • •   –   • –   – •   • •   – • – •

_____ _____ _____ _____ _____ _____ _____

Now try your own hand at Morse code. Write a message in code and give it to a partner to decipher.

Name _____

A Matter of Life and Death

Study the bar graph. It shows how many passengers died and how many survived. Then answer the questions.

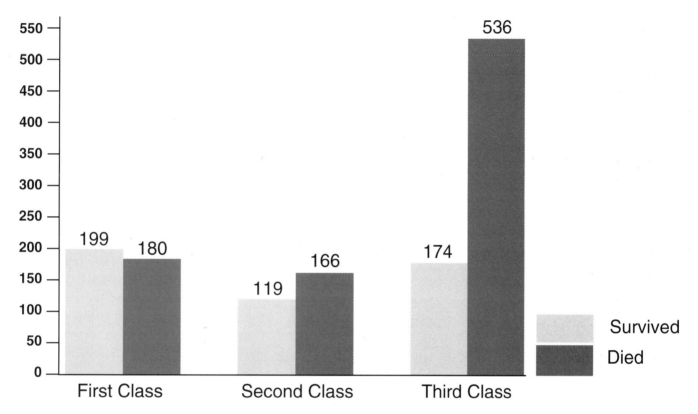

1. In total, how many passengers died?

   _____

2. What was the total number of passengers who survived?

   _____

3. Which class of passengers had the most survivors?

   _____

4. Which class of passengers had the most deaths?

   _____

5. What conclusions can you draw from the above information?

   _____

25

Now Presenting...

Getting the Scoop on UFOs

Eric is a journalist for his school newspaper. When he hears about a slew of UFO sightings in his hometown, he is overly enthusiastic in his coverage. His journalism teacher has to reel him in and remind him of the basic principles of reporting a story.

Setting the Stage

Background

Engage students in a discussion about UFOs. First, explain that the acronym stands for "unidentified flying object." Strictly speaking, it is applied to any flying object that cannot be conclusively identified or explained. Most commonly, the term is used to refer to spacecraft inhabited by intelligent beings from other planets. Stories about UFOs appear in the news from time to time, and students may have heard of such sightings or encounters. Ask them to share what they know about these reports, and to give their own opinions on the subject of UFOs and extraterrestrial life-forms.

Staging

You may choose to provide the character of Eric with props such as a notepad and tape recorder or microphone.

Encore

Students may wish to investigate the topic of UFOs further after reading this play. If they enter the key word *UFO* in the search engine at a site such as Yahooligans (www.yahooligans.com), they will be directed to a number of fascinating sites where they can learn more. Students may even wish to investigate UFO sightings in their own community.

Vocabulary

Introduce and discuss the following words before reading the script. Make sure students know that some of these words have more than one meaning (the meanings provided here correspond to the way each word is used in the context of this play).

alien: an intelligent being from another planet

colonize: to travel to another planet with the intention of establishing a permanent residence for oneself and others

objective: factual, neutral, without any bias or opinion

outlandish: silly or unbelievable

replicate: to copy or reproduce

sighting: a report of an eyewitness

solar system: the nine planets orbiting around our sun

spacecraft: an aircraft capable of traveling through outer space

universe: everything that exists in space

Now Presenting...

Getting the Scoop on UFOs

When Eric hears about a rash of UFO sightings, he goes all out to get the scoop for his school newspaper.

Characters

Narrator.................................. _____

Eric Hunter .... _____

Mrs. Brown.............................. _____
(Eric's journalism teacher)

Mr. Ortiz .... _____
(the science teacher)

Janet Jameson......................... _____

Mrs. Tomlin .... _____

Mr. Kemper .... _____

Getting the Scoop on UFOs

·················· **Characters** ··················

Narrator   Janet Jameson
Eric Hunter   Mrs. Tomlin
Mrs. Brown   Mr. Kemper
Mr. Ortiz

Narrator: In the town of Glendale, Arizona, there have been a lot of UFO sightings lately. Eric's journalism teacher encourages him to write a story about it for the school newspaper.

Mrs. Brown: Eric, I suppose you've heard about the UFO sightings around town.

Eric: Yeah, isn't that far out? That'd make a great headline for the school newspaper!

Mrs. Brown: That's just what I was thinking. I was wondering if you'd like to write up a story for next week's issue.

Eric: No sooner said than done. This could be a major breakthrough in my career.

Mrs. Brown: Don't get carried away, Eric. Just get the facts. Here's the tape recorder and some batteries. Don't forget to take your pad and extra pens. I want a rough draft on my desk by Friday.

Eric: *New York Times,* here I come!

Mrs. Brown: Oh dear . . .

Narrator: Eric makes his way to the neighborhood where most of the sightings had been reported. A friend of his has suggested he start by talking to a girl named Janet Jameson.

Eric: Do you mind if I ask you some questions about the UFO sightings around here?

Janet: I didn't see too much, but I'll tell you what I know.

Eric: Wait a second while I turn on my tape recorder. Now, just start from the beginning.

Janet: Well, I was in bed last Sunday night trying to go to sleep, but I was just tossing and turning. Then at about 10 o'clock, I saw a red light shining through my bedroom window. That was strange, because my bedroom window is in the back of the house. I got up and looked out. There was a V-shaped thing in the sky. It had small red lights all along the edges. It definitely was *not* an airplane, because it was perfectly still. As soon as I looked at it, the lights went out. I had goose bumps all over!

Eric: And then?

Janet: That's it. It slowly drifted away, and then I went to sleep.

Eric: That's all? I need more than *that* to write a story.

Janet: Go talk to Mrs. Tomlin across the street. I hear she saw it too.

Narrator: To Eric's great relief, Mrs. Tomlin picked up the story where Janet left off.

Mrs. Tomlin: I saw the whole thing as I was coming home Sunday night. It was red and shaped like a triangle, just like Janet said. After the lights went out, it came down near that pasture, directly over a cow. The poor cow must have been scared to death. It was frozen to the spot. A beam of light came down from the UFO and shone on the cow. Then the cow started to float up and into the UFO!

Eric: *Now* things are getting interesting!

Mrs. Tomlin: I wouldn't have believed it if I hadn't seen it with my own eyes.

Eric: What happened after that?

Mrs. Tomlin: The spacecraft just floated away, faster and faster until it was out of sight. Strangely, it didn't make a sound. It was totally silent.

Eric: Why in the world would aliens from another planet want to steal a cow?

Mrs. Tomlin: Don't ask me. The whole thing is over my head. You might ask Mr. Kemper down the block. He's a UFO nut. I'm sure he could fill in some of the blanks.

Narrator: In a matter of minutes, Eric was knocking on Mr. Kemper's door. The elderly man was more than glad to give Eric a lecture about UFOs.

Mr. Kemper: There are a lot of things we don't know about our universe, young man. Take our solar system, for example. How many planets are there?

Eric: There are nine planets in our solar system. I learned that in science class.

Mr. Kemper: Think again. There are actually 10 planets. The 10th one is known as Planet X. It's far beyond Pluto. That's where the aliens are from.

Eric: Why are they coming here? And why are they stealing cows?

Mr. Kemper: They want to steal our DNA.

Eric: Our what?

Mr. Kemper: DNA is like a set of instructions for growth. It tells the cells how to grow to form a cow, for example, or a sea star. The aliens are studying the DNA on Earth. Maybe they want to replicate this life on another planet. Or maybe they want to colonize the Earth. Who knows? The only thing for sure is that they're here, and we'd better get used to it.

Eric: Thanks, Mr. Kemper. This is going to be the biggest story ever!

Narrator: Eric took his notes and tapes and wrote a story about the sightings in Glendale. He was so excited that he wrote the whole thing from start to finish without stopping. The next day, he proudly placed his article on Mrs. Brown's desk. She read it slowly and carefully. Much to Eric's surprise, she was not impressed.

Mrs. Brown: Eric, you can't be serious! Did I read this correctly? Aliens are coming to Earth from Planet X to collect DNA? Who told you all these things?

Eric: I have all the sources in my notes.

Mrs. Brown: You have to admit, this is pretty outlandish.

Eric: C'mon Mrs. Brown. Have an open mind. Just because it's a little weird doesn't mean it can't be true.

Mrs. Brown: That's not the problem. You have confused fact and opinion. Do you know the difference?

Eric: A fact is something that is true, and an opinion is a personal thought or belief.

Mrs. Brown: Correct. According to the witnesses, a UFO was seen in Glendale, and it supposedly kidnapped a cow. Personally, I don't believe it. But that's not the point. You should explain who said what. It's a fact that your witnesses said those things. It's not necessarily a fact that those things happened. As a journalist, you have a responsiblity to let your readers make up their own minds.

Eric: Journalists aren't allowed to give opinions?

Mrs. Brown: It's OK to give opinions, but you should let the reader know it's an opinion. And another thing: You should present several different points of view. Why don't you talk to Mr. Ortiz, the science teacher? He might be able to give another point of view that will help you round out your story. Then you can write another draft. I know there's a good story in here somewhere.

Narrator: Later that day, Eric interviewed Mr. Ortiz in his classroom. He didn't buy the UFO story.

Mr. Ortiz: I believe that your witnesses saw something, but was it really a UFO? It could have been a lot of different things.

Eric: Like what?

Mr. Ortiz: It could have been stars shining through the haze. It could have been low-flying aircraft. You might check with the airport to see what kinds of aircraft were flying through the area that night.

Eric: Good idea. What do you think of the Planet X theory?

Mr. Ortiz: That seems rather far-fetched to me. If this planet is far beyond Pluto, as Mr. Kemper says, it would be incredibly distant from the Sun, and therefore freezing cold. Too cold for life, I would think.

Eric: Thanks, Mr. Ortiz. You've really made me think about this a little more closely. I think I'm ready to write a more objective article.

Mr. Ortiz: Good luck.

Narrator: Eric finished the second draft of his article and turned it in to Mrs. Brown on Friday.

Mrs. Brown: Good job, Eric. This is a very interesting report. You used the witnesses' own words to report on what they saw. And you gave several different explanations. I think you learned an important lesson in journalism.

Eric: I sure did. I still believe in UFOs myself, but I'll let my readers make up their own minds about it.

Name _____

Facts and Opinions

Read the following statements. Write **F** next to statements that are facts according to the script. Write **O** next to statements that are opinions.

1. _____ Many people in Glendale claim they saw a UFO.

2. _____ UFOs are unidentified flying objects.

3. _____ Mrs. Tomlin said she saw a UFO kidnap a cow.

4. _____ The UFO is from Planet X.

5. _____ Planet X is the 10th planet in our solar system.

6. _____ DNA is a set of instructions for cellular growth.

7. _____ The aliens want our DNA.

8. _____ Mr. Ortiz said the UFO was really just light shining through the haze.

9. _____ No other planet in this solar system could possibly support life.

10. _____ Pluto is very cold because it is so far from the Sun.

Write four statements of your own about the script. Two statements should be facts. Two statements should be opinions. Ask a friend to write **F** or **O** next to your statements. Discuss the answers.

1. _____

   _____

2. _____

   _____

3. _____

   _____

4. _____

   _____

Name _____

Both Sides of the Argument

Do you believe in UFOs? What are some good arguments for and against their existence? Give three reasons to support believing in UFOs and aliens, and three reasons not to believe in them. An example has been provided for you.

Reasons to Believe in UFOs	Reasons Not to Believe in UFOs
The universe is vast. The odds are high that there's another planet with intelligent life.	All the conditions necessary for life have to coexist. One or two conditions may coexist on many planets. But, it's highly unlikely that all conditions are met on one planet as on Earth.

Now Presenting...

The Montgomery Bus Boycott

In one simple act of defiance, Rosa Parks began a historic boycott. When Martin Luther King, Jr., joined the boycott, the Civil Rights movement began.

Setting the Stage

Background

With students, discuss the era of segregation in the United States. Make sure they are aware that during the first half of the twentieth century, black Americans were not allowed to go to the same schools as whites. They could not eat in restaurants with white people or live with them in the same neighborhoods. The facilities provided for blacks were, for the most part, substandard and designed to humiliate them. In the South, segregation was not merely a custom—it was the law. People who violated these laws could be arrested and jailed. In the 1950s blacks began to defy these laws in ever-increasing numbers. Perhaps the most well-known instance is that of Rosa Parks, who refused to give up her bus seat for a white man. Her subsequent arrest resulted in a year-long bus boycott in Montgomery, Alabama, which was led by the Reverend Dr. Martin Luther King, Jr.

Staging

For the bus scene, you might use masking tape to outline an area of the stage in the shape of a bus and arrange chairs for the readers within that area.

Encore

After reading this play, students may enjoy reading Rosa Parks' story in her own words. *I Am Rosa Parks* is an illustrated book that is suitable for reluctant readers. Ms. Parks also wrote another version of her autobiography for more fluent readers entitled *Rosa Parks: My Story.*

Vocabulary

Use the following words from the script to enrich your discussion about the Civil Rights movement:

arrest: to stop and hold someone by the power of law

boycott: to not use a service as a form of protest

desegregate: to end an official policy of separation of the races

despair: lack of hope

fine: an order to pay money as punishment

fingerprint: to cover a person's fingertips with ink and then press them onto paper to identify or keep track of that person

humiliation: a feeling of deep embarrassment or shame

injustice: unfair or wrongful treatment

justice: the righting of a wrong

nonviolence: use of a peaceful approach

racist: a person filled with hatred for people of other races

Now Presenting...

The Montgomery Bus Boycott

In 1955 a woman by the name of Rosa Parks refuses to give up her bus seat for a white man. This simple act leads to a year-long boycott within the black community of Montgomery, Alabama.

Characters

Narrator.................................... _____

Rosa Parks .... _____

Bus Driver .... _____

Police Officer........................... _____

Mrs. Pratt .... _____

Raymond Parks .... _____

E.D. Nixon............................... _____

Martin Luther King, Jr. .... _____

Crowd...................................... _____

_____

_____

The Montgomery Bus Boycott

.... **Characters** ....

Narrator	Raymond Parks
Rosa Parks	E.D. Nixon
Bus Driver	Martin Luther King, Jr.
Police Officer	Crowd
Mrs. Pratt	

....

Narrator: It is Thursday, December 1, 1955. A black woman named Rosa Parks is waiting at a bus stop on Cleveland Avenue in Montgomery, Alabama. When the bus stops for her, she boards the bus and takes a seat in the back, where blacks are required to sit. After several other stops, the front seats are all filled up with white people, and one white man is standing in the aisle.

Bus Driver: You back there, get up! I need those seats . . . Did you hear me lady? I said get up . . . Are you going to move or not?

Rosa: No, I'm not.

Bus Driver: You must not be hearing right, lady. Everybody knows those seats go to white folks when they're needed. You know I'm not going to be able to let you get away with this. . . What would all my passengers think? There's a law about this, you know.

Rosa: Maybe it's time we had a law that treated people fairly.

Bus Driver: I'll let someone else worry about whether the laws are fair or not. Lady, I'm calling the police to have you arrested.

Rosa Parks: You do that.

Bus Driver: *(stopping bus, opening door, and shouting)* Excuse me, officer. Could you please step on the bus and help us out?

Police Officer: *(boarding bus)* What's the problem?

Bus Driver: This lady won't get up and give her seat to the other passenger. I told her to move, but she won't budge.

Police Officer: Do you speak English, lady?

Rosa: Yes, I do.

Police Officer: Did you understand what the bus driver said?

Rosa: Yes, I did.

Police Officer: Then why won't you get up?

Rosa: I didn't think I should have to. Why do you push us around?

Police Officer: I don't know. But the law is the law and you're breaking it. I'm putting you under arrest.

Narrator: The police officer put Rosa into a patrol car and took her to jail. She was fingerprinted and photographed, and then she was put into a cell. A friend of Rosa's, Mrs. Pratt, had been on the bus when Rosa was arrested. She ran to Rosa's house to tell her husband what had happened.

Mrs. Pratt: Rosa didn't move. The bus driver had to pull the bus over and call the police. The next thing I knew, Rosa was on her way to jail!

Raymond: I'm going to need some help. Go get my friend E.D. Nixon. Tell him to meet me at the jail, and quick!

Mrs. Pratt: Whatever you say, Raymond!

Narrator: Raymond and E.D. paid Rosa's bail and got her out of jail. When they got home, they all discussed Rosa's arrest over a cup of coffee.

Raymond: They didn't hurt you, did they?

Rosa: No, but I almost got another fine! I was so thirsty that I just drank out of the water fountain at the jailhouse without paying any attention. The officer told me the fountain was for whites only. Imagine that—even in jail!

E.D.: It's time for change. We've been living with this injustice for *too* long. I think that your arrest might be a blessing in disguise, Rosa.

Rosa: Why do you say that?

E.D.: Word about your arrest is going around town like wildfire. The people are up in arms about it. This is our chance to organize the community.

Raymond: How?

E.D.: We can boycott the buses! If we have to give up our seats to white people, we shouldn't ride the buses at all.

Rosa: How long will the boycott last?

E.D.: Until they desegregate the buses.

Raymond: E.D., we can't change the whole world in one day.

E.D.: But we've got to start *somewhere.* Are you with me?

Rosa: Yes, E.D. It's time, like you said.

Raymond: Rosa, I'm worried about your safety. You know a lot of whites are going to be mighty mad when they hear about this.

Rosa: If we all unite, we can be strong and help each other get through this.

Narrator: Later that night, E.D. planned the boycott with a new minister at the Dexter Avenue Baptist Church. The new pastor's name was Martin Luther King, Jr.

E.D.: This boycott is going to need a lot of organization. We'll need a place to come together and coordinate our efforts. I'm suggesting we use the church as a meeting place. I was hoping you could provide some leadership, Reverend King.

King: I'm not sure that's such a good idea. I've only been here for a year. The people may not accept me as a leader.

E.D.: The situation is never going to be perfect. We all just have to rise to the occasion and do the best we can.

King: I can see the urgency of the situation. Yes, let's use the church as our headquarters. How do you think we should handle the boycott?

E.D.: Volunteers have already made leaflets telling people not to ride the buses on Monday. We've also set up some car pools so that people can still get to work, and black cab drivers have agreed to give people rides for 10¢.

Narrator: On Monday, December 5, there were hardly any black people on the buses. Instead, they gathered on street corners and waited for rides from friends and cab drivers. Rosa went to court and was fined $10 for breaking the law. She refused to pay the fine. That night, there was a mass meeting to decide on a future course of action. At the meeting, Reverend King was elected leader of the movement. He gave a speech that electrified his audience.

King: We are here because we are American citizens, and we are determined to apply our citizenship to the fullest.

Crowd: That's right!

King: There comes a time when people get tired of being trampled. There comes a time, my friends, when people get tired of being subjected to humiliation and despair.

Crowd: Tell it!

King: We have a long road ahead of us, brothers and sisters. Our enemies will try to bring us down into the pit of hatred. You cannot have hatred in your heart and seek justice at the same time. We must meet violence with nonviolence.

Crowd: Show us the way!

King: Right here in Montgomery when the history books are written in the future, somebody will say, "There lived a race of people, of black people, who had the moral courage to stand up for their rights."

Crowd: It's true!

King: In the meantime, we must stick together and work together if we are to win our rights as Americans. The boycott will continue, for what we are doing is right. What we are doing is just.

Crowd: God bless you, Brother King.

Narrator: The blacks of Montgomery were determined to stand up for their rights and to challenge white power. They continued the boycott in spite of threats and attacks by racists. On December 20, 1956, the U.S. Supreme Court finally ordered the City of Montgomery to desegregate its buses. The boycott had lasted over a year, but it had achieved its goal. Blacks no longer had to give up their seats to white passengers. Reverend King continued to fight for justice, and growing numbers of people joined him in his struggle. Rosa Parks' simple act of defiance one year earlier had marked the beginning of what is now called the Civil Rights movement.

Cause and Effect

Complete the table below to show how causes and effects are linked together in the play. The first one has been done for you.

Cause	Effect
Rosa refuses to give up her seat on the bus for a white man.	The bus driver calls the police.
Rosa still refuses to get up, even when the police officer tells her to.	
	Raymond goes to the jailhouse with his friend E.D.
E.D., Rosa, and Martin Luther King, Jr., join forces to organize their community.	
The first day of the boycott is a success, and Reverend King steps up as a leader.	
	Montgomery must desegregate its buses. Blacks no longer have to give up their seats to white passengers.

Name _____

Martin Luther King's Vision

Martin Luther King, Jr., was a key figure in the Civil Rights movement. He provided a new vision for the future. Read this quote from one of his speeches. Then tell what the quote means to you. What is your dream of the future?

I have a dream that my four children will one day live in a nation where they will not be judged by the color of their skin but by the content of their character.

_____

_____

_____

_____

_____

_____

Now Presenting...

All the Rice in India

An elephant trainer wants to marry the Rajah's daughter. To win the Rajah's approval, he must prove himself to be clever and resourceful.

Setting the Stage

Background

Tell students that the play they are about to read is based on a folktale from India. Point out India on a world map. Explain that India is a modern democracy, but that it was once ruled by rajahs. A rajah was like a king and had absolute power. Many folktales from India tell how certain rajahs misused this power and were then taught a lesson on how to be more fair. In this play, the Rajah's greed is put in check by a humble, yet clever man.

Staging

You may wish to provide a chessboard and a small amount of rice to use as props in this story. Students may use the chessboard to measure out the first few moves in the trainer's math riddle.

Encore

Students may enjoy reading other versions of this folktale, including the classic *One Grain of Rice* by Demi, and *The Rajah's Rice* by David Barry.

Vocabulary

Introduce the following words, and then ask students how they think these words might be used in a folktale about an elephant trainer who wants to marry a princess.

caretaker: a person who tends to another person's (or animal's) needs

embedded: to be stuck inside surrounding material

infected: to be full of germs or bacteria

medicinal herb: a plant with the power to heal

nuisance: a bother

outwit: to trick or fool somebody

pierce: to puncture or go through

resourceful: good at knowing what to do in different situations

wound: a cut or gash in flesh

Now Presenting...

All the Rice in India

Arjun is in love with Chahna, the Rajah's daughter. The problem is that Arjun is an elephant trainer, and the Rajah surely won't approve of their marriage. How can Arjun prove himself worthy?

Characters

Narrator .... _____

Chahna .... _____

Arjun .... _____

Rajah .... _____

Guard .... _____

Advisor .... _____

     Readers' Theater, Grade 5 • EMC 3310

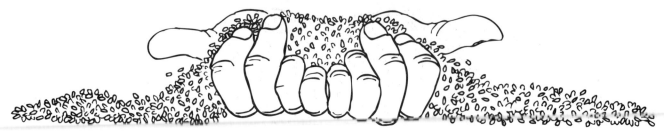

All the Rice in India

················· **Characters** ·····················

Narrator	Rajah
Chahna	Guard
Arjun	Advisor

···

Narrator: In a small village in India a long time ago, there lived a man by the name of Arjun. Arjun was a caretaker for the Rajah's elephants. He was in love with Chahna, and Chahna was in love with him. They planned on getting married, but they had to keep it a secret. Chahna was the Rahja's daughter, you see, and if he knew the princess was in love with an elephant trainer, he would have thrown a royal tantrum. Every morning, Arjun and Chahna met each other and talked by the elephant yard.

Chahna: Arjun, what are we to do? My only dream is to be with you, but my father will forbid it.

Arjun: I will prove myself to him. The Rajah will see that I am worthy to be the husband of his one and only daughter.

Chahna: He's not that easy to impress, as you know. In fact he seems to be more stuck in his ways than ever.

Arjun: I know. He has demanded one bag of rice from every villager, even though we barely have enough for ourselves. I wish he could see how we suffer.

Chahna: We will find a solution, dear one. Where there is love, there's a way.

Arjun: One of the messengers is coming! Let us pretend that everything is normal.

Guard: *(entering)* Good morning, Princess. Are you ready for your morning stroll?

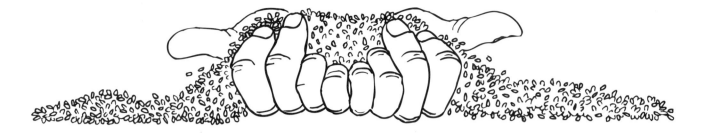

Chahna: Yes, Arjun was getting Ganesha ready for me.

Messenger: She's a grand elephant, isn't she?

Chahna: Yes, she is. She's my favorite, as a matter of fact. I've been riding her ever since I was a child. *(to Arjun)* I will bring her back later today.

Arjun: Yes, Your Highness.

Narrator: The next day, Chahna came to the elephant yard bright and early, as usual. To her surprise, Ganesha would not get up. She just lay on the ground with her eyes half closed. The sight of this threw Chahna into a panic.

Chahna: Arjun, what's wrong with Ganesha?

Arjun: She must have fallen ill. She was like that when I got here this morning.

Chahna: *(crying)* Arjun, you must do something. Ganesha is like a sister to me.

Arjun: Don't cry, Chahna. Ganesha will be all right. I'll see to her myself.

Narrator: Ganesha did not move for the rest of the day. Arjun inspected every inch of her body. Finally, he noticed a spot on her foot where a sharp thorn had pierced her thick hide and become embedded in her flesh. The wound had become infected. He ground up some medicinal herbs and packed the mixture around the cut. In a few days, Ganesha was back on her feet.

Advisor: Your Majesty, I bring good news.

Rajah: What is it?

Advisor: Ganesha has been healed.

Chahna: Thanks be to all the gods and goddesses!

Advisor: Actually, you can thank Arjun the elephant trainer. It was he who cured Ganesha.

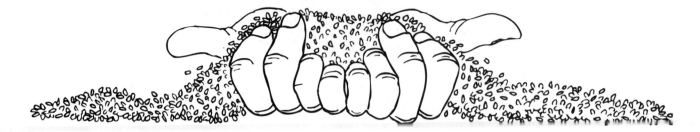

Rajah: Please bring Arjun here. I would like to thank him myself.

Advisor: He is in the next room, Your Majesty. I knew you would want to speak with him. *(louder)* Arjun, you may enter.

Arjun: *(entering)* Good afternoon, Your Majesty. *(bowing toward Chanha)* Greetings, Your Highness.

Rajah: I would like to thank you for healing Ganesha. Chahna loves that elephant dearly, and Chanha's happiness is dear to me. Therefore, I owe you my happiness. Name your reward.

Arjun: I don't ask for much. Just a grain of rice.

Rajah: That's all? You can have anything you want, and all you ask for is a grain of rice?

Arjun: All right, then. If it pleases Your Majesty, you may give me a single grain of rice today. Tomorrow you can give me two grains of rice. On the following day, give me four grains of rice. For 30 days, give me double the rice you gave me the day before.

Rajah: That hardly seems to be a worthy reward. But if that is your wish, you shall have it.

Narrator: On the next day, Arjun received two grains of rice. The following day, he received four grains of rice. On the fourth day, he received eight grains of rice. The amount doubled every day. On the 10th day, it had only come to 512 grains of rice. The Rajah was amused.

Rajah: *(to his advisor)* Arjun may have a gift for handling animals, but he certainly isn't so clever with numbers. He could have had anything he wanted, and all he asked for were a few measly grains of rice.

Advisor: To be sure. Today is the 11th day. A messenger gave him 1,024 grains of rice.

Rajah: And so tomorrow we will give him 2,048 grains of rice.

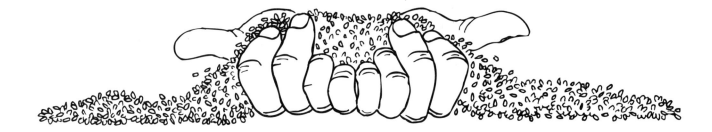

Advisor: Correct.

Rajah: It sounds like a lot, but it only adds up to a couple handfuls of rice. I guess he will learn his lesson the hard way.

Narrator: On the 16th day, Arjun received 32,768 grains of rice. That was enough to fill a bag. On the 17th day, two bags of rice were delivered. On the 18th day, he got four bags. The Rajah was getting slightly concerned.

Rajah: Tell me, how much rice did we give Arjun today?

Advisor: I'm afraid that this is beginning to add up, Your Majesty. Yesterday, we gave Arjun two bags of rice. And today, we gave him four bags of rice.

Rajah: And eight bags tomorrow.

Advisor: And 16 bags the day after that.

Rajah: I know how to count! Now be gone!

Narrator: On the 27th day, the situation was getting serious.

Messenger: Your Majesty, today we have to deliver 2,048 bags of rice to Arjun. It's too much for us to carry. We need to use Your Majesty's elephants.

Rajah: Go ahead. Out of curiosity, what does all this add up to tomorrow?

Messenger: It will be 134 million . . .

Advisor: . . . 217 thousand . . .

Chahna: . . . 728 grains of rice.

Advisor: Or, in other words, one whole storehouse of rice.

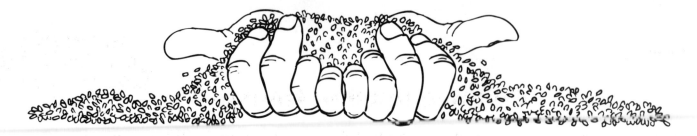

Rajah: This added up to more than I thought. But there are only three more days to go. Then this whole nuisance will be over with.

Advisor: But we're dealing with bigger numbers now. Tomorrow we must deliver two full storehouses of rice. On the next day...

Rajah: Just tell me what it comes to on the 30th day.

Advisor: It comes to 536 million, 870 thousand, 912 grains of rice. That is more than we have, Your Majesty.

Rajah: I see that one grain of rice can indeed add up to a lot. Arjun is much more clever than I thought. Bring him to me at once.

Advisor: Yes, Your Majesty.

Chahna: Father, there's something you should know.

Rajah: Not now, Chahna. Let me speak to Arjun first.

Arjun: *(entering)* Yes, Your Majesty?

Rajah: Arjun, you have outwitted me. Your request is impossible to satisfy. Name any other reward you want.

Arjun: I ask for your daughter's hand in marriage.

Rajah: How dare you! You think you can trick me into letting you marry my daughter? She is more precious to me than life itself. You can have all the rice in India, but you *cannot* have my daughter.

Chahna: Father, please let us marry. I am in love with Arjun, but I didn't know how to tell you.

Rajah: Chahna, you know I cannot deny you. If you want to marry Arjun, so be it. He has proven himself to be clever and resourceful. May you both live happily ever after.

Name _____

Comprehension Questions

How well did you understand this play? Write your answers to the questions in the spaces provided.

1. What is the problem at the beginning of the play?

   _____

   _____

2. What kind of person is the Rajah?

   _____

3. What is wrong with Ganesha, and how does Arjun help her?

   _____

   _____

4. What does Arjun want for his reward?

   _____

   _____

5. What does the Rajah think of Arjun's request?

   _____

6. Why do you think Chahna didn't tell the Rajah about her plans to marry Arjun?

   _____

   _____

7. What do you think is the moral or lesson of the story?

   _____

   _____

Name _____

Rice and More Rice!

How many grains of rice did the Rajah have to give Arjun each day? Write the missing numbers to complete the chart.

Day 1	Day 2	Day 3	Day 4	Day 5
1	2	4	8	16
Day 6	**Day 7**	**Day 8**	**Day 9**	**Day 10**
32	64	128		
Day 11	**Day 12**	**Day 13**	**Day 14**	**Day 15**
1,024		4,096		
Day 16	**Day 17**	**Day 18**	**Day 19**	**Day 20**
32,768				524,288
Day 21	**Day 22**	**Day 23**	**Day 24**	**Day 25**
1,048,576		4,194,304		16,777,216
Day 26	**Day 27**	**Day 28**	**Day 29**	**Day 30**
	67,108,864		268,435,456	

Readers' Theater, Grade 5 • EMC 3310

Now Presenting...

Enter Bruce Lee

Bruce Lee was an awe-inspiring figure who is still respected today for his hard work, dedication, and creativity. His mission in life was to introduce the world to the wisdom of the Chinese culture.

Setting the Stage

Background

Tell students that the play they are about to read is a biography of Bruce Lee, a martial artist and actor. Explain that Lee was born in San Francisco, but he moved to Hong Kong with his parents at a very young age. There he was introduced to kung fu and became increasingly skilled at this martial art. By the time he returned to the United States in his early 20s, he was ready to open his own kung fu studio. In time, he opened three different studios in California. Some of his clients included famous actors and other celebrities.

Eventually, Lee decided to become an actor himself, working first in television in the *Green Hornet* action series. When he sought leading roles on the big screen, Bruce found that Hollywood was not ready for a Chinese leading man. He moved back to Hong Kong, where his film career soon took off. Within a few short years, Lee was directing and starring in his own films. His last full-length film, *Enter the Dragon,* was hugely successful in the United States. He began another film called *The Game of Death* but died while filming it. The cause of death has never been determined. Students might ask their parents what they know about Lee, whether they ever saw him on television in *Green Hornet,* or whether they ever saw the popular TV show, *Kung Fu,* based on Lee's idea about a kung fu master in the Old West.

Staging

You might draw a five-tiered pagoda on the board. The student playing Bruce Lee can point to different parts of the drawing as he delivers his lines to Kareem Abdul-Jabbar in the final scene.

Encore

Encourage students to research the lives of other athletes, actors, or artists that they admire. They may then use this information to write their own biographical plays about these inspirational figures. Books in the series by Kathleen Krull provide many short and humorous synopses of such individuals. Titles include *Lives of the Athletes: Thrills, Spills (And What the Neighbors Thought); Lives of the Musicians: Good Times, Bad Times (And What the Neighbors Thought);* and others.

Vocabulary

Introduce and discuss the following words before reading the script:

cha-cha: a modern Latin American ballroom dance

instrumental: helpful in causing something to happen

kung fu: a Chinese system of self-defense that emphasizes circular movements; praying mantis and wing chung are kung fu styles

martial art: one of any of the systems of self-defense, including kung fu, judo, and karate

philosophy: a system of beliefs and practices for guiding your life

postpone: to put off or delay

prejudice: a judgment or an opinion formed without knowledge of the facts, including a negative opinion of people with different racial backgrounds

spar: to box with jabbing movements

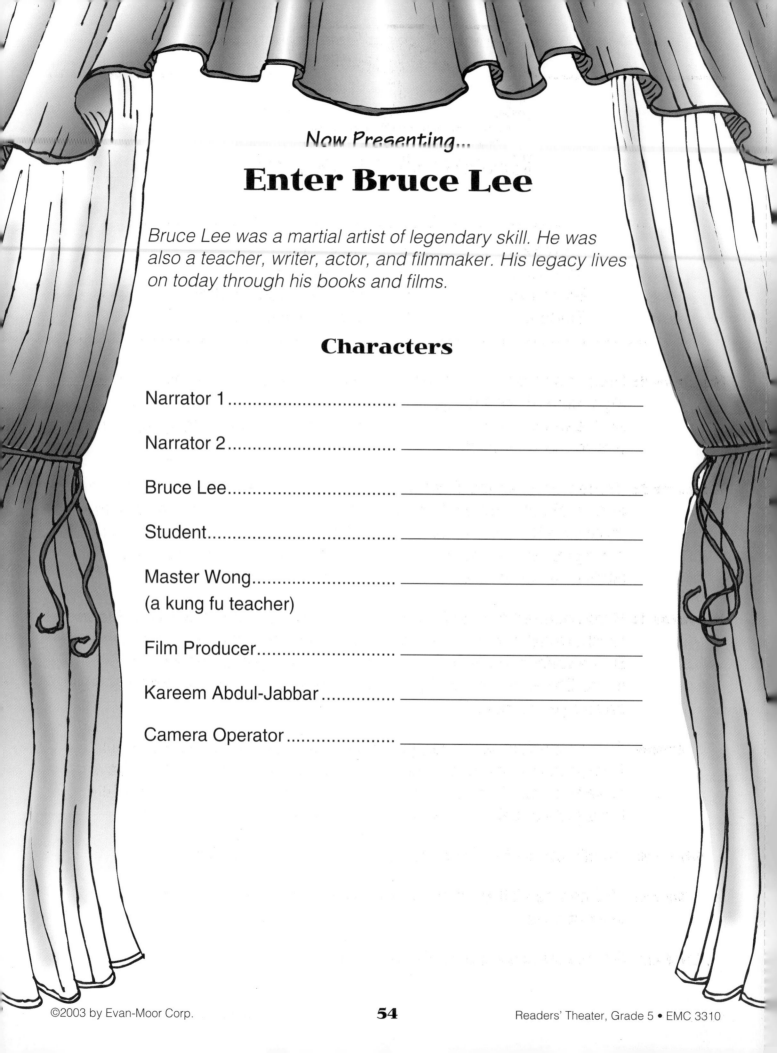

Now Presenting...

Enter Bruce Lee

Bruce Lee was a martial artist of legendary skill. He was also a teacher, writer, actor, and filmmaker. His legacy lives on today through his books and films.

Characters

Narrator 1 .... _____

Narrator 2 .... _____

Bruce Lee .... _____

Student .... _____

Master Wong .... _____
(a kung fu teacher)

Film Producer .... _____

Kareem Abdul-Jabbar .... _____

Camera Operator .... _____

Enter Bruce Lee

···················· Characters ····················

Narrator 1	Master Wong
Narrator 2	Film Producer
Bruce Lee	Kareem Abdul-Jabbar
Student	Camera Operator

Narrator 1: Bruce Lee was an awesome martial artist. His skill and precision are legendary. Even though he died in 1973, people still watch his films and read his books. He was an instrumental figure in bringing martial arts to the United States.

Narrator 2: Bruce wasn't so tough as a young man, though. In fact, he was sickly and weak. He took up kung fu to protect himself as a teenager, but mostly he liked to dance. He even became the Hong Kong cha-cha champion at the age of 18. Later, when he moved to the United States, he focused on kung fu and made it his life.

Narrator 1: Bruce opened a kung fu studio in Oakland, California. Many Chinese teachers did not want to share their knowledge with westerners, but Bruce welcomed people of all colors. This angered some people in the Chinese community. Some people came to the studio to challenge his ideas.

Bruce: To be an effective fighter, you have to be a master of your own self. Everybody wants to rule the world, but nobody wants to learn the art of self-control. That's what this style of kung fu is all about, you see. It's a path of self-discovery and self-expression.

Student: What's this style of kung fu called? Does it have a name?

Bruce: You can call it the art of fighting without fighting. It's a style without style.

Student: So that means I can do whatever I want to do?

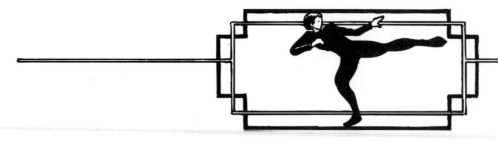

Bruce: Not exactly. Just empty your mind and flow with the present moment. You have to be like water, my friend. Water can take any shape at all. If you pour it into a cup, it's a cup. If you pour it into a teapot, it's a teapot. Be like that.

Master Wong: *(entering)* Are you Lee?

Bruce: Some people call me that.

Master Wong: *(to the student)* Who are you?

Student: I'm one of Mr. Lee's students.

Bruce: And who are you?

Master Wong: I'm also a teacher of kung fu. People told me you are teaching our secrets to white people, and now I can see it's true.

Bruce: This knowledge is to be shared with the world. The ancient masters would agree.

Master Wong: You don't have any authority to say these things. I and others have decided that you had better close your studio and go somewhere else.

Bruce: And what if I don't?

Master Wong: Let's make a deal. You and I will spar. If I win, you have to stop teaching kung fu to whites. If you win, then you can do whatever you want and nobody will bother you.

Bruce: It's a deal.

Narrator 2: As they were preparing to spar, Master Wong sensed Bruce's power. Suddenly he wanted to postpone the fight. Bruce insisted they settle the matter right then and there. Wong got scared and started running around the studio. Bruce threw him to the floor, and Wong had to admit defeat.

Narrator 1: Bruce's reputation began to grow. He developed his own style of kung fu, called jeet kune do, and opened two more studios. Soon he was even charging movie stars as much as $200 dollars an hour for private lessons. Then to everybody's surprise, Bruce closed all three of his studios.

Narrator 2: Bruce decided that he wanted to introduce Americans to martial arts and Chinese philosophy. He thought the best way to do this would be through films. He starred in several TV shows, and began to work on his own movie scripts at home. During his days in Hollywood, Bruce discovered that there was a great deal of prejudice against Asians.

Producer: Good morning, Mr. Lee. Please take a seat.

Bruce: Thank you.

Producer: An assistant showed me some footage of you in action. I have to say I'm very impressed. Actually, we have you in mind for a new TV series.

Bruce: What's it called?

Producer: It's called *Green Hornet.* You would play a character named Kato. Right now we're producing a show called *Batman.* It's still very new, and we can't tell if it's going to be successful or not. So, we can't really start on *Green Hornet* quite yet. We would probably start the show next year. Could you wait that long?

Bruce: I suppose I could wait. In the meantime, would you mind looking at this script I wrote?

Producer: Sure. What's it about?

Bruce: It's about a kung fu master who travels through the Old West. You know, cowboys and all that. He runs into all sorts of trouble, but he always remembers the words of his teacher. The lessons from his old master are told through flashbacks. It's a good way of getting in little bits of Chinese philosophy.

Producer: We will certainly take a look at it.

Narrator 1: Bruce *did* wind up in *Green Hornet,* and it was a great success. He made other appearances on TV as well, but he was never able to get a starring role. A TV producer took his idea for the *Kung Fu* TV series, but he didn't want to take a chance on a Chinese actor for the starring role. Instead, the producer hired a white actor to play the role of the kung fu master.

Narrator 2: Bruce was so disappointed that he decided to move back to Hong Kong, where he grew up. There he starred in a film called *The Big Boss,* which was a smash in China. Other films quickly followed. Over the years he produced, directed, and starred in films such as *Fist of Fury* and *Enter the Dragon.* Bruce returned to Hollywood to make his final film *The Game of Death.* It co-starred Kareem Abdul-Jabbar, a major U.S. basketball star. Kareem used to be one of Bruce's kung fu students, so the two worked very well together.

Abdul-Jabbar: So what's the last scene in the movie supposed to be about?

Bruce: My character comes to rescue a treasure hidden at the top of a pagoda. The pagoda has five levels, and there are guards at all five levels. Each guard is a master of a different kind of martial arts style. I have to fight my way to the top of the temple to get the treasure.

Abdul-Jabbar: What are the different styles?

Bruce: The first one is a kind of kicking style. It's very fast and direct.

Abdul-Jabbar: What about the second level?

Bruce: You can call that one the Chinese level. The guard is a master of the praying mantis style and wing chung.

Abdul-Jabbar: And the others?

Bruce: They're blends of different styles—Japanese kenpo, nunchaku, and my own jeet kune do. The guardian on the fourth floor is a seventh-degree black belt. You play the role of the guardian at the highest floor of the pagoda. Since you're on the highest floor, you represent the highest level of skill.

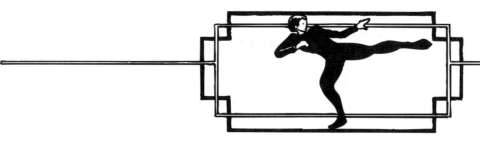

Abdul-Jabbar: Now I'm listening.

Bruce: I knew you'd be perfect for this part. You fight with an unknown style. This is the essence of a true master. He can adapt to any situation, any style.

Camera Operator: Excuse me, Mr. Lee. We're ready to start filming.

Bruce: All right, Kareem. Let's go. We'll start by facing each other from opposite ends of the room. When the film starts rolling, forget the script. Just flow with the moment.

Camera Operator: Lights! Camera! Action!

Narrator: Kareem approached Bruce slowly and intensely. They eyed each other like two tigers. Kareem's leg shot out from the side like a bolt of lightning. Bruce flew through the air in a blur.

Camera Operator: Cut!

Bruce: What's the matter? Wasn't that good?

Camera Operator: I don't know. I couldn't see it!

Abdul-Jabbar: What do you mean?

Camera Operator: You guys were moving too fast for the film to catch the movement. Can you slow it down just a little bit?

Narrator 2: Bruce's performance in *The Game of Death* was phenomenal. It was one of the most amazing displays of physical coordination ever captured on film. Sadly, his fans would never get to see it in its entirety. Bruce died under mysterious circumstances before the film was completed.

Narrator 1: Today, Bruce is respected as an inspiring teacher and a man of many talents. He dedicated himself to his art form and wanted to share his knowledge with others. Many young athletes today are inspired by his words to do their best and to follow their own truth.

Name _____

The Man and the Legend

What did you learn about Bruce Lee? Fill out the diagram to show what you know.

What he thought about different styles of martial arts:

_____

_____

How he felt about his cultural heritage:

_____

_____

His achievements in the martial arts:

_____

_____

His skills in the film industry:

_____

_____

Name _____

Coming Soon to a Theater Near You

If you were a filmmaker or producer, what kind of film would you make? Would it be an action film? Who would star in it? What role would that actor play? Write your ideas in the spaces provided.

Title of Film: _____

Category: _____

Director: _____

Cast: _____

Characters: _____

Setting: _____

Summary of Plot: _____

_____

_____

_____

_____

_____

_____

Now Presenting...

Haste Makes Waste

When Alex paints his room without taking the necessary precautions, he drips paint all over the carpet. Now he's going to have to take responsibility for his mistake and make enough money to pay for the damage.

6 parts

Setting the Stage

Background

Responsibility and work ethic are important topics in this play. Ask students what it means to take responsibility for one's actions. What would they do if they made a mistake that cost another person money? Is it enough to simply say you're sorry? Why or why not? You might also talk about the steps involved in a job well-done: planning, preparation, execution, and checking one's work. Talk about these steps in the context of a variety of different jobs or tasks.

Staging

For the scene in which they are looking through the want ads, You may choose to provide a newspaper for the students playing the roles of Alex and Laura.

Encore

How realistic are the job opportunities and pay rates given in this play? Have students look through the want ads of your local newspaper to see what kinds of jobs or training programs are available for young people in your community.

Vocabulary

Introduce and discuss the following words before reading the script:

haste: trying to be quick; hurrying

tarp: short for *tarpaulin,* a piece of waterproof canvas cloth, often used to cover or protect other things

waste: to make poor use of something; worthless material, fit to be thrown away

Haste Makes Waste

Preparation is a necessary step in any job or task. Unfortunately, Alex is going to have to learn that lesson the hard way.

Characters

Narrator.................................. _____

Alex .... _____

Laura...................................... _____

Mr. Turner .... _____

Mrs. Turner .... _____

Mr. Wright .... _____

63

Haste Makes Waste

····················· **Characters** ·····················

Narrator	Mr. Turner
Alex	Mrs. Turner
Laura	Mr. Wright

Narrator: Alex lives at home with his family. He has a large, sunny bedroom all to himself. The problem is, he hates the color. It's too bright, and it gives him a headache. So, he's decided to repaint it himself. As he gets ready to start, his parents give him some last-minute tips and instructions.

Mrs. Turner: Do you need anything, dear?

Alex: Thanks, Mom. I think I've got everything I need. Take a good look at these old walls. You won't even recognize this place next time you see it!

Mr. Turner: Just make sure that you lay a tarp down on the floor and put sheets over the furniture.

Mrs. Turner: And don't forget to put masking tape around the windows.

Alex: Don't worry. I'll do a good job.

Mrs. Turner: You're sure you don't want any help?

Alex: Positive.

Mrs. Turner: All right, then. We'll be in the backyard working on the garden. Call us if you need anything. *(Mr. and Mrs. Turner leave.)*

Laura: *(entering)* Good morning, Picasso. Getting ready to paint your masterpiece?

Alex: I sure am. Wanna help me stir the paint?

©2003 by Evan-Moor Corp.   **64**   Readers' Theater, Grade 5 • EMC 3310

Laura: Shouldn't you have something covering the floor? And what about the furniture? You haven't even moved it away from the wall.

Alex: I haven't got time for all that. I want to get this finished in time to go to the movies later on today.

Laura: Remember what they say: "Haste makes waste."

Alex: And "Time is money." That's another proverb for you. Speaking of which, I'd better get started. The clock is ticking!

Laura: You'd better not get paint on anything.

Alex: Don't worry, I'll be careful.

Narrator: Alex painted his whole room in less than two hours. He splattered paint all over the carpet in the process. At the rate he was going, it's a wonder he didn't get paint on the furniture too. When his parents came to check in on him, they were not amused.

Mrs. Turner: Alex, this is a disaster. Just look at this carpet!

Mr. Turner: Didn't we tell you to put a tarp down?

Alex: Yeah, but . . .

Mr. Turner: No ifs, ands, or buts about it. We let you do this by yourself under the condition that you do it properly.

Mrs. Turner: Now what are you going to do?

Alex: It doesn't bother me. I just won't look at it.

Mrs. Turner: Well it bothers us, and this is *our* house.

Alex: I suppose I'll have to replace the carpet. Now that I look at it, I can see that I need to tidy up the paint job on some of these walls too.

Mr. Turner: That would be the responsible thing to do.

Mrs. Turner: I guess you'll have to get a part-time job. You don't have enough money of your own to buy a new carpet.

Alex: How much does a new carpet cost?

Mr. Turner: You'll have to figure all that out yourself. Here's the telephone book.

Narrator: To Alex's great shock, he learned that it would cost over $300 to replace the carpet! Added to the cost of the paint, the whole project would come to about $400. Alex's new dilemma was how to earn all that money. His sister helped him look through the want ads in their local newspaper.

Laura: This one says they're looking for a dog-sitter.

Alex: What does a dog-sitter do?

Laura: Watch dogs, silly.

Alex: That sounds boring. Keep looking, please.

Laura: *(pointing to an ad)* Oh, how about this one?

Alex: *(reading ad)* A house painter? You must be kidding!

Laura: Well, at least you know how it's *not* done. You could put that on your application.

Alex: Very funny.

Laura: I don't see anything else in here. It's worth a try, Alex. I hear that house painters make good money.

Alex: Did I hear money?

Laura: As in ka-ching!

Alex: Would you hand me the telephone?

Narrator: Alex got an interview set up for the very next day. He was eager to show his parents that he could be responsible. The painter's name was Mr. Wright.

Mr. Wright: Can you tell me what you know about painting?

Alex: Well, I know that preparation is half the job. You have to be sure to put something down on the floor and tape the window frames. If you don't, you might get paint on something. And that would be a disaster.

Mr. Wright: Have you had any jobs before?

Alex: Well, not exactly . . .

Mr. Wright: I'm sorry, but we're looking for somebody with some previous experience with painting and carpentry.

Alex: When I said that I've never had a job, I meant that I'd never had a paid job. I've actually done a lot of different jobs at home. You can ask my parents. They've taught me a lot about how to do things the right way.

Mr. Wright: Well, since you put it that way, perhaps we could make an exception. You know that this is just a part-time job through the summer, right?

Alex: That suits me perfectly, since I have to go back to school in September anyway.

Mr. Wright: All right, then. It's settled. I'll see how you do tomorrow.

Narrator: That night, Alex told his family the good news at the dinner table.

Alex: I gave you and Dad as my references, so Mr. Wright might call you tonight.

Mr. Turner: He already did, as a matter of fact. We told him that you're a good worker who is willing to learn from his mistakes.

Alex: Thanks, Dad.

Laura: How much are you going to make?

Alex: I'll make $7 an hour. How long will it take me to make enough money for carpeting and paint for the room?

Mrs. Turner: Calculate it. How many hours a week will you work?

Alex: Three hours a day, five days a week. That's 15 hours a week.

Mr. Turner: Now multiply 15 hours per week by $7 an hour.

Alex: That's $105 a week. So, I can earn $420 in one month. That'll do it.

Narrator: Alex soon became a wonderful apprentice painter. After four weeks, he had enough money to buy a new carpet and the necessary supplies to repaint his room. He didn't know how to trim the carpet by himself, so he let his father help him. Alex repainted the room by himself, taking all the necessary precautions, of course!

Mrs. Turner: Your room looks lovely, Alex. I like the way the colors all go together.

Alex: I wasn't really thinking about it, but I guess you're right.

Mr. Turner: I'm proud of the way you took responsibility for your mistake, son.

Alex: I guess I learned my lesson: Haste makes waste.

Laura: Now that you've paid for the carpet and paint, are you going to quit the job, Alex?

Alex: No, I like having my own money. I'll have to quit in September when school starts, but I think Mr. Wright will hire me again next summer. I think he can use the help during the summer months, and he says he's happy with my work.

Mr. Turner: As I said when he asked, you really know how to learn from your mistakes! You've turned pain into profit!

Name _____

Problems and Solutions

Alex had a lot of different problems along the way, but he worked them all out. Show how he solved his problems by completing this table.

Problem	Solution
Alex hates the color of his bedroom.	
	He decides to pay for the carpet and paint supplies.
He doesn't have any money.	
	He uses his parents as references.
He doesn't know how to trim carpet.	

 Readers' Theater, Grade 5 • EMC 3310

Name _____

Words from the Wise

This play has several different proverbs in it. **Proverbs** are very old sayings. They often give advice on practical matters. What do you think the proverbs below mean? Rewrite them in your own words.

1. Haste makes waste.

_____

_____

2. Time is money.

_____

_____

3. Better safe than sorry.

_____

_____

4. The early bird catches the worm.

_____

_____

5. A penny saved is a penny earned.

_____

_____

6. Money doesn't grow on trees.

_____

_____

7. Nothing ventured, nothing gained.

_____

_____

70

Now Presenting...

Journey to a New World

Ioscoda and two of his friends are kidnapped by French explorers and taken to meet the king. Everything they see along the way appears other-worldly.

Setting the Stage

Background

Introduce this play by summarizing some important ideas related to the exploration and settlement of North America. Using a map, explain that English settlers established colonies in what is now called New England. Meanwhile, French explorers were establishing colonies of their own in Canada and the Great Lakes region. At first, these explorers were not hostile to the native peoples they encountered. It was in their interest to establish friendly relations with them. In some cases, however, they abducted Native Americans and took them back to Europe. Oral accounts of these abductions circulated among Native Americans and, over the years, took on the quality of a myth or legend. This play is based on a folktale from the Ottawa tribe, which was established on the northern shores of Lake Huron.

Staging

You may want to mark off areas on the floor to represent the three scenes of action: the shoreline, the ship, and the king's court.

Encore

Students may want to compare this folktale to other accounts of contact between Europeans and Native Americans. The story of Squanto, a Pawtuxet who served as a cultural liaison, is told in *Squanto: A Warrior's Tale.* This live action film is available on video and is rated PG.

Vocabulary

Introduce and discuss the following words before reading the script:

cabin: an enclosed room on a ship

expanse: a huge area

motion: to make a gesture

mutually beneficial: something that is favorable or positive for both people

quest: a journey in search of something

suspicion: a feeling of not trusting someone or something

token: a sign or symbol

Journey to a New World

Ioscoda and two of his friends are on a quest to find the home of the sun. Instead, they are taken against their will to a strange new world.

Characters

Narrator.. _____

Ioscoda .... _____

Assikinack .... _____

Blackbird .... _____

Captain.. _____

Shipmate.. _____

King... _____

 Readers' Theater, Grade 5 • EMC 3310

Journey to a New World

······················· **Characters** ·······················

Narrator	Captain
Ioscoda	Shipmate
Assikinack	King
Blackbird	

Narrator: Many, many years ago, Ioscoda and his friends decided to go on a journey. They wanted to find the home of the sun. They knew it would be toward the east, because the sun rises in the east every day. After traveling for one full cycle of the moon, they at last came to a vast expanse of blue water.

Blackbird: This is the largest lake I have ever seen. It goes on and on as far as the eye can see.

Ioscoda: *(sniffing the air)* There is an unusual smell. Taste the water, Assikinack.

Assikinack: *(smacking his lips)* Blecch! The water is salty! It's no good for drinking.

Blackbird: Salt water? Strange indeed. This must be the entrance to the home of the sun. How will we cross it?

Ioscoda: If we keep walking around the shore, surely we will come to the other side. *(startled)* Look! Do you see that?

Assikinack: Yes, it looks like a floating island, and it's coming this way. What should we do?

Ioscoda: We will wait here until the island reaches the shore. Then we will see what happens next.

Narrator: As the island came closer and closer, Ioscoda and his friends could see strangely dressed beings moving to and fro on it. When it touched land, the strange beings walked from the island onto the shore over a short bridge.

Blackbird: Behold! Visitors from the land of the sun! Even their hair is made of gold.

Assikinack: Don't be so sure, Blackbird. I sense danger. We should go back.

Ioscoda: Be brave, Assikinack. Let us go meet them and see what this is about.

Narrator: The three young men walked toward the strange beings. They all came face to face on the beach. It was an electrifying moment. They eyed each other with a great deal of curiosity and more than a little suspicion. When they began to speak, each group had to guess what the other was saying based on their gestures and body language.

Captain: We come in peace. Please join us on our ship.

Blackbird: What is he saying?

Assikinack: He's pointing to the island. I think he wants us to go to the island with him.

Captain: *(to Shipmate)* They don't understand us. Give them a necklace and then motion again toward the ship.

Shipmate: Please accept this gift. It's made of gold and jewels. We have other gifts we want to give you on the ship.

Ioscoda: Ship?

Shipmate: Yes! The ship! *(pointing)* Over there. Come, this way.

Assikinack: Don't go. It's a trick.

Ioscoda: I want to know where they're from. Yes, they are strange and somewhat silly, but I don't think we are in any danger. Not yet, anyway.

Narrator: They all boarded the ship and went into one of the cabins. There the captain served Ioscoda and the others food that they had never tried before. Then they were presented with more gifts.

Captain: *(handing a mirror to Ioscoda)* This is a token of friendship from our king.

Ioscoda: It's like a sheet of ice on the water, but it's not cold. Look, you can even see your breath on it.

Blackbird: Now there are two of you, Ioscoda.

Captain: The king wants very much to establish friendly relations between our nations.

Ioscoda: King?

Shipmate: *(to Captain)* He's quick.

Captain: *(murmuring)* Yes, I think the king will be very pleased with our catch.

Assikinack: Yakkety yak yak. Enough of all this nonsense! We're leaving—now!

Narrator: When they went back up on deck, however, they saw that the ship was surrounded by water. The captain had given orders to set sail while they were in the cabin. Ioscoda, Blackbird, and Assikinack did not know what to think, so they simply waited and looked for clues to help them understand what was happening to them. Every morning they rose early to see if they had reached the home of the sun.

Blackbird: Ioscoda! Assikinack! We've already reached land. This must be the home of the sun.

Assikinack: It's not the land of our fathers, that is certain.

Ioscoda: Do you see the houses? They look to be made of stone.

Blackbird: And the people go about on sledges pulled by elk without horns. This is all like a dream.

Assikinack: Nowhere are there others like us. This cannot be the home of the sun.

Captain: *(entering)* Welcome to France. Tomorrow we will meet the king, so you'd better be on your best behavior. The future depends upon it. Oh, and by the way, put on some of these clothes. You can't go see the king looking like *that. (shouting)* Ready on the deck! Aim! Fire!

Blackbird: *(covering his ears)* What was that? It sounded like thunder.

Ioscoda: Smoke is coming from those black logs. It must be their way of announcing our arrival.

Narrator: The next day, the captain, Ioscoda, Assikinack, and Blackbird were all gathered before the king.

Captain: *(gesturing to Ioscoda)* This one seems to be their leader, Your Majesty. He's a smart one too. He learned a lot during our voyage. You'll find he can understand most everything you say.

King: *(to Ioscoda)* What is your name, kind sir?

Ioscoda: My name is Ioscoda. This is Assikinack, and this is Blackbird. They are my friends.

King: I see. I compliment you all on your bravery. You have traveled a very great distance. When you return, I hope you will give your chief my greetings. You will hear more from us in the near future. I hope you will receive us as well as we have received you.

Blackbird: Who is he, and what did he say?

Ioscoda: I think he's their chief. He said we're going back.

Assikinack: It's about time.

King: Here are some gifts we would like you to give to your chief. Take them as a token of friendship. We hope that this will lead to a mutually beneficial relationship.

Narrator: Ioscoda bowed deeply upon receiving these gifts. He and his companions boarded a ship the very next day and journeyed back to the land of their birth. The three travelers had endless discussions about whether they had really traveled to the home of the sun. One thing was certain. They knew that the strange beings would come back to visit them again one day. Ioscoda and his people looked forward to that day with a great deal of curiosity and more than a little suspicion.

Name _____

Look Again

Everything looked very strange to Ioscoda, Assikinack, and Blackbird during their trip to Europe. Show what they were really looking at by completing this chart.

What It Looked Like	What It Really Was
a huge lake	
a floating island	
a sheet of ice	
a sledge	
an elk without horns	
a smoking log	

Name _____

What Were They Thinking?

Fill in the thought bubbles to show what different characters in the play thought about each other.

Ioscoda

Captain

King

Assikinack

Now Presenting...

Women in Science

Chelsea decides to create a multimedia presentation for the school science and technology fair. Her presentation—which includes "portraits" of Marie Curie, Rachel Carson, and Sally Ride—wins honorable mention for its originality.

Setting the Stage

Background

Ask students if they have ever been to a science fair and, if so, what it was like. Share with students that a science fair is an opportunity for scientists and inventors to exhibit their experiments or inventions. There are often educational exhibits at these fairs as well that present the work of other scientists from the past. Invite students to brainstorm a list of ideas for an exhibit at a science fair. Tell them that this play is about a girl who decides to make a presentation aimed at educating people about women in science.

Staging

You may wish to press the "play" button on an empty tape recorder or make a clicking sound before students playing the parts of Marie Curie, Rachel Carson, and Sally Ride read their lines.

Encore

Students may want to learn more about Marie Curie, Rachel Carson, Sally Ride, or another scientist of interest. Encourage students to create monologues using information from their research. They may deliver a report to the class in the first person, saying, for example, "My name is Sir Isaac Newton."

Vocabulary

Review these words and their meanings with students. Then ask how these words might be used at a science fair:

atom: the tiniest part of an element that has all the properties of that element

ecosystem: the interconnected relationship between all forms of life and the natural resources in a particular environment

molecule: the smallest part of a substance that displays all the chemical properties of that substance

multimedia: consisting of two or more media, such as print and recorded sound

nucleus: the inner core of an atom

nutrient: proteins, minerals, vitamins, and other substances that provide nourishment

pesticide: a chemical used to kill unwanted insects or plants

radiation: gamma rays released from radioactive material

Now Presenting...

Women in Science

For a science and technology fair, Chelsea decides to create a presentation on women in science. Her presentation pays respect to those women who have opened the door for others.

Characters

Narrator.. _____

Ms. Bryant...................................... _____

Chelsea.. _____

Moses .... _____

Gino .... _____

Marie Curie .... _____

Rachel Carson .... _____

Sally Ride....................................... _____

Women in Science

····················· **Characters** ·····················

Narrator	Gino
Ms. Bryant	Marie Curie
Chelsea	Rachel Carson
Moses	Sally Ride

Narrator: Chelsea, Moses, and Gino are all classmates in biology. At the end of class, their teacher makes an announcement about an upcoming science fair.

Ms. Bryant: Oh, and by the way, there's going to be a science and technology fair in March. At the fair, presenters can exhibit an original experiment, or they can showcase the work of another scientist. Everybody is encouraged to participate.

Chelsea: *(whispering)* You know that "everybody" means boys.

Ms. Bryant: What was that, Chelsea?

Chelsea: I was just saying that the science fair might as well be for boys only. You never see any girls there.

Gino: That's because there aren't any women scientists.

Ms. Bryant: Oh yes there are. You don't hear about them as often, but they certainly have made some important contributions.

Chelsea: Name one female scientist.

Ms. Bryant: I can name more than one. Marie Curie discovered radium, for example. Then there's Rachel Carson, a pioneer in the conservation movement. More recently, there was Sally Ride. I'm sure you've heard of her.

Chelsea: The astronaut?

Ms. Bryant: That's right. She was a scientist on board the *Challenger* space shuttle. So don't tell me there haven't been any female scientists. Now, if you're interested in hosting a booth at the fair, your proposal has to be submitted in two weeks. Class dismissed!

Moses: I can't wait to get started on my proposal. I think I'll do a model of Alexander Graham Bell's first telephone. What about you, Gino?

Gino: I'm not sure, but I might try to make a robot.

Chelsea: I think I'll create a presentation on women in science.

Moses: What?

Chelsea: That's right. We hardly ever hear about women making a mark in the world of science. Like Ms. Bryant said, though, women have made some important contributions. I want to help spread the word about some of their work!

Gino: Well, good luck doing your research.

Moses: Yeah—I bet you're really going to have to dig.

Chelsea: Well, I'm ready!

Narrator: That weekend, Chelsea got started on her project. She decided to do multimedia "portraits" of the three women scientists she learned about in class. First, she downloaded information and pictures from the Internet showing the scientists at work. She gathered scientific instruments, tools, and other objects related to their fields of study. At the fair, she organized all these materials at a booth to create her three portraits.

Gino: Chelsea, I can't wait to see your project. Everybody's talking about it.

Chelsea: Well, here it is. Want me to give you the official tour?

Moses: Definitely.

Chelsea: At my booth, I'm showcasing the work of three female scientists. I've created three different stations. Each one is a kind of portrait of the scientist. The first one I'd like to introduce to you is Marie Curie.

Gino: Who's that? Is she the one who invented radar?

Chelsea: Not radar, *radium.* Just push the tape button and listen to the recording.

Gino: Multimedia, eh? Nice touch.

Narrator: Gino pushed the "play" button on the tape machine. They all listened to the recording while studying the items on display.

Curie: My name is Marie Curie. I discovered radium in the early 1900s. For this discovery, I earned the Nobel Prize for physics in 1911. I was also a pioneer in the medical uses of X rays.

Moses: I've got a question: Why can X rays show what's underneath our skin?

Chelsea: Shh—Keep listening.

Curie: All matter is made up of molecules. Molecules, in turn, are made up of even smaller particles called atoms. The atoms in radium are so active that they release electromagnetic energy at special frequencies. This energy can pass through body tissues and produce a photographic image.

Moses: Oh, so *that's* why.

Chelsea: Unfortunately, Marie didn't know about the harmful effects of radiation. She was exposed to massive amounts of radiation because of her work and became very ill.

Gino: No wonder you have to wear a lead vest when you go to the dentist.

Chelsea: Exactly—radiation can't go through lead. And now for my next portrait. Fellow classmates and colleagues, I would like to introduce you to Rachel Carson.

Narrator: Chelsea guided Gino and Moses to the next station. Seashells, dried bits of seaweed, and sand were arranged in a tray to represent life at the shore. On the bulletin board was a picture of a woman exploring a tide pool. Chelsea played another tape, and it was almost as if the woman in the photo were speaking to them.

Carson: Plants and animals coexist in their environment in harmony. The complex relationship between all these forms of life and resources is called an ecosystem. Take a sea star, for example. When it dies, its body breaks down and mixes together with other plant and animal matter on the ocean floor. This mixture becomes a rich source of nutrients that provide food for other creatures. As you can see, these forms of life are all connected together. If one link in the chain is damaged, other links are affected too.

Chelsea: Rachel showed how pesticides affect this chain. In the next part, Rachel is going to talk about the dangers of chemical pesticides.

Carson: Chemical pesticides are absorbed into plants. Insects that eat these plants absorb the chemicals too. The chemicals are then passed on to birds when they eat those insects. It has been shown that DDT, a powerful pesticide, causes the eggshells of some birds to become very thin. This has led to a decline in many bird populations.

Narrator: As Gino and Moses listened, Chelsea pointed to different parts of a diagram she had created on the bulletin board. The diagram showed how different plants and animals are connected together in a food chain.

Moses: Wow, Chelsea. That's really interesting! I suppose that's why there is a ban on lots of different pesticides now.

Chelsea: Luckily, we've learned from our mistakes. People didn't know about the dangers of pesticides before Rachel did her research. The next and final scientist in my presentation is Sally Ride. She was America's first female astronaut. Let me play this video tape for you. It shows Sally floating onboard the space shuttle *Challenger*.

Narrator: The video showed a curly-haired woman floating in the cabin of a spaceship. She spoke to the audience through a headset.

Ride: This is one of the coolest jobs you could ever have. Sure, it's a lot of work. I have to launch and repair satellites, test equipment, and so on. But the thing I'll remember most about this flight is how fun it was. In fact, I'm sure this is the most fun I'll ever have in my life!

Chelsea: See? Science doesn't have to be all work and no play.

Gino: And it definitely *isn't* just for men.

Narrator: At the end of the fair, Chelsea received a special award during the closing ceremonies.

Ms. Bryant: I would like to present an honorable mention to Chelsea Holmes for her project showcasing the work of women in science. Chelsea showed a great deal of ingenuity and creativity in her project. And she was able to connect scientific concepts to larger social issues, an area which isn't often explored. Congratulations, Chelsea.

Chelsea: Thank you very much, Ms. Bryant. In my project, I wanted to pay respect to those women who have paved the way and opened the door for others. Women have made very important contributions in the field of science and continue to do so. In the past, women were limited only by a lack of opportunity, not by a lack of capability. With the increased opportunities available today, we can make even greater contributions than ever!

Women in Science

What kind of symbol would you create for each of the women scientists in this play? Draw a picture of the symbol on each computer screen. Then label the symbol and tell why you chose it.

Marie Curie

Symbol: _____

Reason: _____

_____

_____

Rachel Carson

Symbol: _____

Reason: _____

_____

_____

Sally Ride

Symbol: _____

Reason: _____

_____

_____

Name _____

Word Sort

Sort the following words and terms into the three categories shown. If you need to, use a dictionary for help.

astronaut	atom	ecosystem
food chain	molecule	nucleus
pesticide	satellite	space shuttle

Astrophysics	**Biology**	**Physics**
_____	_____	_____
_____	_____	_____
_____	_____	_____

Now write a short paragraph using the words from one of the categories.

_____

_____

_____

_____

_____

_____

_____

_____

_____

Now Presenting...

Tall Tales from the Wild West

Five colorful characters from American folklore sit around a campfire and try to impress each other with renditions of their exploits.

Setting the Stage

Background

Tell students that tall tales are sometimes called "the fine art of exaggeration." Stories of outlandish escapades are an important tradition in American folklore. Ask students if they have ever heard of Davy Crockett or his wife Sally Ann Thunder Whirlwind Crockett. They may have also heard of John Henry, Pecos Bill, and Paul Bunyan, all of whom are featured in this play. Some characters, such as Annie Oakley, were actual people whose adventures became the stuff of legend. Invite students to share what they know about these or other characters from American folklore.

Staging

You may pile books in the center of the floor and then drape them with an orange scarf to represent the campfire. Have readers sit around the "fire" as they read their lines. They may like to try using a Southern or other regional accent for their part.

Encore

Students may enjoy reading *Sally Ann Thunder Whirlwind Crockett: A Tall Tale* or *Mike Fink*, both by Steven Kellog. Other titles about American folk heroes include *John Henry* by Julius Lester and *Shooting for the Moon: The Amazing Life and Times of Annie Oakley* by Stephen Krensky.

Vocabulary

Introduce and discuss the following words before reading the script:

critters: a slang word meaning "creature" or "animal"

hospitable: friendly and kind toward guests

inclination: interest or desire

spigot: a faucet

tongariferous: amazing; outlandish

varmint: a troublesome person or animal

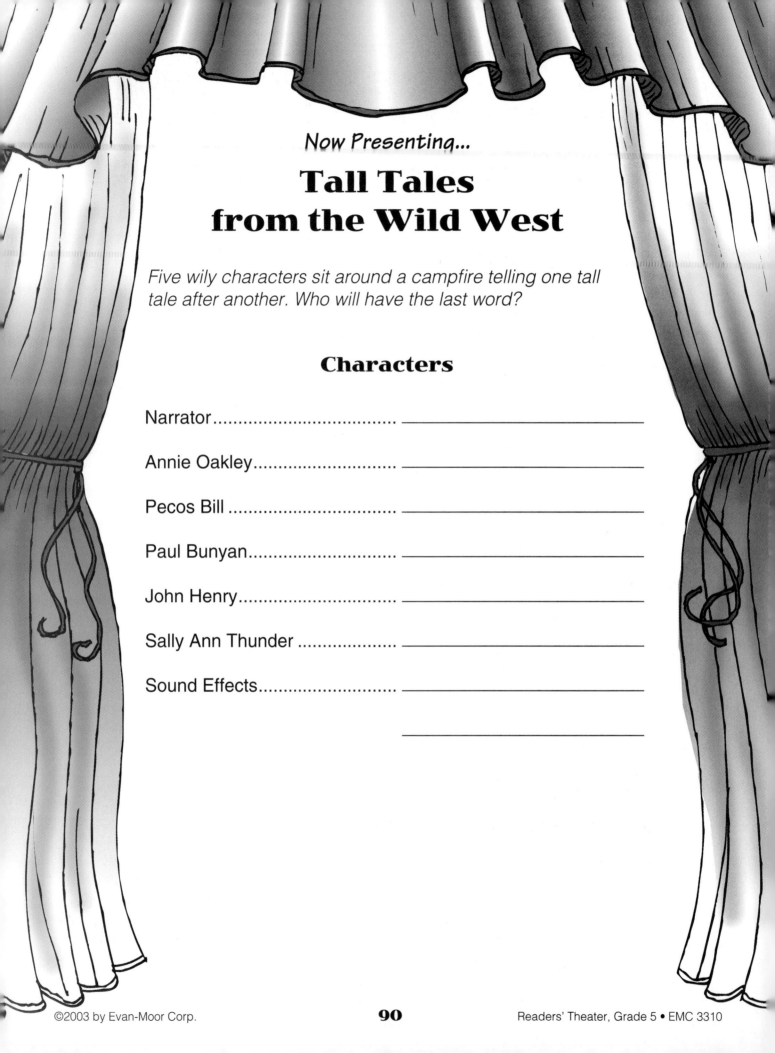

Now Presenting...

Tall Tales
from the Wild West

Five wily characters sit around a campfire telling one tall tale after another. Who will have the last word?

Characters

Narrator .... _____

Annie Oakley .... _____

Pecos Bill .... _____

Paul Bunyan .... _____

John Henry .... _____

Sally Ann Thunder .... _____

Sound Effects .... _____

_____

Tall Tales from the Wild West

·········· Characters ··········

Narrator   John Henry
Annie Oakley   Sally Ann Thunder
Pecos Bill   Sound Effects
Paul Bunyan

Narrator: Gather 'round, guys and gals. Pretend you're sittin' by a campfire out in the desert at night. Rub your hands together by the warmth of the fire. Take a big whiff of the sagebrush and hickory root. Go on, take a whiff. Smell it? You're in for a treat, 'cuz tonight you're gonna hear some tall tales straight from the horse's mouth, so to speak. Without further ado, just sit back and stretch your legs out—and don't believe a thing you hear!

Pecos Bill: Put another log on the fire, Annie. And pour me another cup of coffee while you're at it.

Annie Oakley: Better yet, I'll just shoot a hole in the coffee can.

Sound Effects: Ping!

Annie Oakley: There you go, pardner. Now you got yourself a coffee can with a spigot. Just put your coffee tin right underneath it.

Pecos Bill: Why thank you, Annie. That's mighty hospitable of you.

Paul Bunyan: It sure is quiet. Listen to them critters out there.

Sound Effects: Ahhooooo!

John Henry: Sounds like a mountain lion, don't it?

Sally Ann: That's a coyote if I ever heard one. A mountain lion just purrs like a pussy cat. Now alligators, that's another story. I had a tongariferous fight with a whole gang of 'gators back in Louisiana. Those scaly old toads came creepin' up on my roof one night while I was fast asleep. They thought they had ol' Sally Ann by the tail. But, oh no! I whipped 'em, flipped 'em, and kicked 'em right into tomorrow. It rained 'gators for five whole days after that!

Pecos Bill: That sure sounds like a predicament you got yourself into, Sally Ann. But it still ain't nothin' compared to some of the tangles done come *my* way.

Narrator: Sally Ann put her hands on her hips and spit into the fire—

Sound Effects: Psssssss!

Sally Ann: You don't say?

Pecos Bill: I *do* say.

Sally Ann: Well, why don't you tell us one of your fine tales and let *us* be the judge of it?

Pecos Bill: Don't mind if I do. Take the time I wrestled with a rattlesnake, for example. That rattler came sneakin' up on me just like those 'gators tried sneakin' up on you. I grabbed hold of the varmint and squeezed all the poison right out of it. Then I twisted the snake into a loop lickety-split and caught a Gila monster with it. And *that's* not all! I caught me an eagle too. And a whole herd of cattle. That's how the lasso came to be, just so you know.

Paul Bunyan: Well, split my timber. That's almost as good as the time I chopped down all the trees in North Dakota. I had to pound all the stumps down with my bare fist so they wouldn't stick up.

Sound Effects: Bumf! Bumf!

Paul Bunyan: I was so tired when I walked away that I was draggin' my ax. That ax carved out some mighty big rivers and valleys. They say I even carved out the Grand Canyon with my ax, but that's another story.

John Henry: That's a good one as far as stories go, but did you ever carve through a mountain in a single day?

Paul Bunyan: Can't say I ever had the inclination.

John Henry: Well, I *can* and I *did*. John Henry's the name, and train tracks are my claim to fame. I've laid tracks every which way you can see. One time I came upon a group of men who wanted to build a track through a hunk of mountain. There was a boulder as big as can be smack-dab in the way. So they set a pile of dynamite under it and—

Sound Effects: Kerboom! Kerbomb!

John Henry: When the smoke cleared, the boulder was still there. It didn't even make a dent. So I swung my hammer up on high and brought it down with all my might.

Sound Effects: Chink!

John Henry: And I brought it down again—

Sound Effects: Chink!

John Henry: And again!

Sound Effects: Chink!

John Henry: I think you get my drift. Anyhoot, before you could say thunderin' tarnation, the boulder was gone. The boss-man was hoppin' like a hornet in love. He said he got a new machine called a steam drill. It could hammer faster and harder than 10 men, accordin' to him, and it never had to stop or rest.

Sound Effects: Phooey!

John Henry: That's what I said. He was trying to get my goat and I knew it. But I was chompin' at the bit to teach that old windbag a lesson, so I made a bet that I could dig a hole through the mountain faster than his darn steam drill. Next day, Mr. Boss-man put me on one side and the steam engine on the other. "The first one to the middle is the winner," he said. I'll let you all have three guesses as to who won—and the first two guesses don't count!

Annie Oakley: That's a mighty fine story, John Henry. You all *talk* nice. Right nice, indeed. I'm a woman of few words, myself.

Narrator: With that, Annie picked up her rifle, aimed it up at the sky, and—

Sound Effects: Tshuuuuu!

Sally Ann: Great balls of fire! She done shot a hole in the moon!

Annie Oakley: They don't call me Little Miss Sure Shot for nothin'!

Narrator: Annie blew the smoke off the barrel of her rifle and leaned against a cactus. Then she picked a thorn out of the cactus, put it between her teeth, and said...

Annie Oakley: ...Got anything to top that?

Narrator: Sally Ann looked at Paul Bunyan. Paul Bunyan looked at Pecos Bill, and Pecos Bill looked at John Henry. Then they ran out of people to look at, so they all just plain ran. And that's the end of this here tale.

Sound Effects: Yip-ee-i-eeeeee!

Name _____

American Folk Heroes

What do you remember about the characters from this play? Complete the word web by writing one or two things about each character.

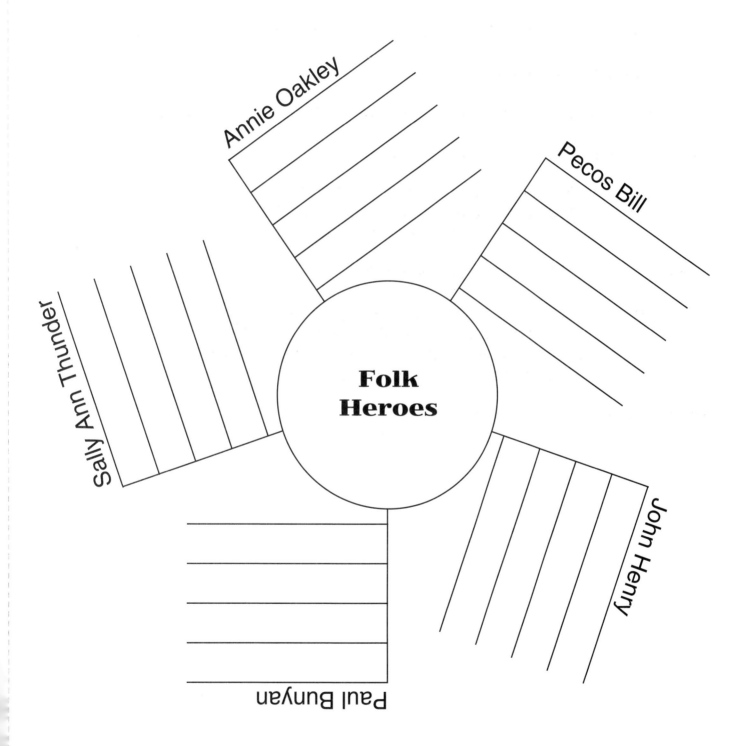

Annie Oakley

Pecos Bill

Sally Ann Thunder

Folk Heroes

John Henry

Paul Bunyan

Name _____

Figuratively Speaking

The characters in this play use a lot of **idiomatic** expressions. Idioms are several words put together that mean something different than what each word means all by itself. Write the following idioms from the play in your own words.

1. Tonight you're gonna hear some tall tales straight from the horse's mouth.

_____

2. Those 'gators thought they had ol' Sally Ann by the tail.

_____

3. I whipped 'em, flipped 'em, and kicked 'em right into tomorrow.

_____

4. Train tracks are my claim to fame.

_____

5. The boulder was gone before you could say thunderin' tarnation.

_____

6. The boss-man was hoppin' like a hornet in love.

_____

7. I was chompin' at the bit to teach that old windbag a lesson.

_____

Name _____

Comparisons

Comparisons are expressions that contrast one thing with another. They make descriptions easier to "see." Study the examples, and then make up some comparisons of your own.

A mountain lion purrs quietly. ➝ *A mountain lion purrs like a pussy cat.*

John Henry was strong. ➝ *John Henry was as strong as 10 men.*

Sally Ann Thunder made a lot of noise. ➝ *Sally Ann Thunder made more noise than a tornado.*

1. John Henry worked hard. ➝ _____

_____

2. Paul Bunyan had big hands. ➝ _____

_____

3. Sally Ann Thunder had a bad temper. ➝ _____

_____

4. Pecos Bill was a good wrestler. ➝ _____

_____

5. Annie Oakley had steady nerves. ➝ _____

_____

6. Paul Bunyan's ox was a big animal. ➝ _____

_____

7. Sally Ann Thunder was tough. ➝ _____

_____

Now Presenting...

Writing on the Wall

A wall on the east side of school is off-limits because it attracts graffiti and troublemakers. The students in Mr. Tomei's art class come up with an idea for replacing the graffiti with an uplifting message.

7 parts

Setting the Stage

Background

Lead a discussion with students about leaders and community heroes. First, ask students what they know about the following leaders and heroes: Martin Luther King, Jr., Princess Diana, Mohandas "Mahatma" Gandhi, Harriet Tubman, and César Chávez. Outline the accomplishments of these leaders. Then brainstorm a list of qualities that they embody. Suggest to students that one of these qualities is that of service to the community. None of these heroes sought personal glory or material gains. They humbly wanted to serve their communities and improve the lives of their fellow human beings. Conclude the discussion by asking students to think of ways that such leaders can be honored and remembered. This play is an original story about a class who decides to honor their favorite heroes in their own way.

Staging

Students may "paint" a wall in the classroom with dry paintbrushes as they deliver their lines in the next-to-last scene of the play.

Encore

Students may want to find out more about the heroes and leaders mentioned in the play. Have them conduct research on a leader of their choice and then make a presentation about him or her to the class.

Vocabulary

Introduce and discuss the following words before reading the script:

prep: abbreviated form of *prepare*

eyesore: something that is unattractive in appearance

P.A.: abbreviation of "public address system"; a system for broadcasting sound in a public place

prime: excellent; good quality

primer: a type of paint used as an undercoat before applying new paint to a surface

unveil: to formally uncover or present a work of art

Now Presenting...

Writing on the Wall

Students in Mr. Tomei's art class turn an eyesore of a wall into an inspiring message.

Characters

Narrator.................................... _____

Principal .... _____

Mr. Tomei.................................. _____

Hugo .... _____

Shawna .... _____

Jennifer .... _____

Derek .... _____

Writing on the Wall

···················· **Characters** ····················

Narrator   Shawna
Principal   Jennifer
Mr. Tomei   Derek
Hugo

Narrator: It's another Monday morning at Brookline Middle School. Hugo, Shawna, Jennifer, and Derek are in their art class, listening to the principal's announcements over the P.A. system.

Principal: Good morning, everybody. Today is Monday, December 15th. It's 50 degrees outside, so all members of the Polar Bear Club are welcome to meet on the playground during recess. And speaking of recess, I have an important announcement. The east side of the school next to the wall is strictly off-limits until further notice. Over and out.

Hugo: That's a shame.

Shawna: It was bound to happen.

Mr. Tomei: Hugo and Shawna, would you like to include the rest of us in your conversation?

Hugo: We were just saying how messed up it is about the east wall.

Mr. Tomei: Messed up because of all the stuff that goes on there, or messed up that it's off-limits?

Hugo: Both, I guess.

Mr. Tomei: For some reason, that wall has always been a magnet for trouble. We don't have enough teachers to supervise all the grounds, and we can't afford to keep repainting every time that wall gets hit by graffiti vandals.

Jennifer: That wall is really an eyesore. The school should do something about it.

Derek: C'mon, Jennifer. Some of that graffiti is cool.

Hugo: Jennifer's got a good point, though, Derek. The graffiti seems like it's a way of saying "Back off!"

Mr. Tomei: Maybe that's the solution.

Hugo: What?

Mr. Tomei: Replace the graffiti with a more positive message.

Jennifer: Like a mural!

Mr. Tomei: Actually, that's just what I was thinking.

Shawna: It'll never work.

Derek: Aw, c'mon, Shawna. Don't be such a drag.

Shawna: Think about it. It would just be asking for more trouble.

Mr. Tomei: But we can at least discuss it, can't we? Let's just pretend for a moment. What if we *were* to paint a mural? What would it be about?

Jennifer: It should be about something positive, like you said, Mr. Tomei. For example, it could be about community leaders. People we can look up to for inspiration.

Hugo: Yeah, like Martin Luther King, Jr. He led the Civil Rights movement in the '50s and '60s. My mom and pop were in the March on Washington. We have his picture in our living room.

Mr. Tomei: Martin Luther King, Jr., is an excellent example of a community leader. Who else can you think of?

Derek: I'd pick César Chávez. My dad works in a union, and he always tells me that workers today owe a lot to him.

Mr. Tomei: Why is that?

Derek: César started a workers' strike in the early '60s. His goal in life was to help workers stand up for themselves and get fair treatment. He was always leading a boycott or a strike. César gave his life to the people. Now *there's* a leader.

Jennifer: Personally, I'd pick Princess Diana. She could have just enjoyed a life of comfort, but she gave all her time to good causes. Children's causes were her favorite.

Mr. Tomei: That's right. I remember how she used to promote campaigns to end the use of land mines in warfare for the sake of children. She would host really large parties and invite wealthy people to make donations to her causes. She was good at raising money.

Jennifer: But she didn't just do glamorous stuff. Right from the beginning, I remember how she was involved with AIDS patients. That was real risky back in those days, because people didn't want to hear or talk about AIDS. Diana could have used her fame for anything, but she chose to use it for the sake of other people. That's why I admire her so much.

Mr. Tomei: It's interesting. All your ideas show how true leaders don't seek fame or fortune. Instead, they work on behalf of others. They help people to help themselves. Who else fits that definition?

Hugo: Harriet Tubman!

Derek: Mohandas "Mahatma" Gandhi!

Mr. Tomei: Good examples. Those are both people who gave their time and energy to improving other people's lives. Shawna, what about you? Don't you have a hero?

Shawna: This is all crazy. You're talking like this is something we're really gonna do.

Mr. Tomei: Well, Shawna, maybe we really are. What do you think, class?

Hugo: Let's go for it!

Jennifer: Why not?

Derek: Count me in!

Mr. Tomei: The first thing we have to do is get permission from the principal. It'll look a lot better if we have a plan in hand. Let's start by making sketches. We can submit them to the principal along with a schedule and budget.

Narrator: For the rest of the semester, the class worked on sketches and plans for their mural. They calculated how much all the paint and supplies would cost, and presented their idea to the principal as a summer project. To their great relief, the plan was approved. As summer drew closer, they posted notices around school inviting other students to participate. Several weeks into the project, they had a surprise visit.

Hugo: Whew! This is hard work.

Derek: Well, at least we've washed and prepped the wall with primer. I think that was the hardest part.

Jennifer: Now that the outline is on the wall, I can start to imagine what it's going to look like.

Mr. Tomei: I'm really pleased with the number of people who have turned out to help too.

Jennifer: There's just one person I wish were here.

Mr. Tomei: Shawna?

Jennifer: Yeah. She just started drifting away from the class the more we got into the project.

Shawna: *(from behind)* Yeah, well, I was feeling pretty down on myself.

Jennifer: *(surprised)* Shawna! What do you mean?

Shawna: That's right, it's me. It's just that I felt like I was being two-faced. See, *I* was one of the kids who was tagging the wall.

Jennifer: You painted all that graffiti?

Shawna: Me and my partners in crime, so to speak. But I've been hanging out and watching you work. It looks really good, and I think it is gonna make a difference. So I was wonderin' if it's too late to join in.

Jennifer: It's never too late to make a difference, Shawna. Grab a brush and we can talk while we work!

Narrator: More people joined in as the summer went on, and the mural was finished ahead of schedule. On the first day of classes, the principal unveiled the mural at a ceremony attended by all the students.

Principal: This mural is a prime example of how people can work together to make a difference in their community. This wall used to be off-limits. Now it is a very special place that belongs to all of you, because all of you helped to create it. The heroes on this wall were inspiration for the mural because they helped to make their communities better too. The quote at the bottom of the wall summarizes the message very well. To conclude our ceremony, Shawna will read the message aloud for all to hear.

Shawna: In the words of labor leader César Chávez, "Being of service is not enough. You must become a servant of the people."

Name _____

Honorable Mention

The students in Mr. Tomei's art class honored their personal heroes in a mural. Other ways to honor heroes are through stamps, coins, postcards, sculptures, and public monuments. How would you honor your personal hero? Fill out the planning form below, and then draw a sketch of your memorial.

Name of Hero: _____

Accomplishments: _____

Admirable Qualities: _____

Idea for Memorial: _____

Name _____

Steps in the Process

What are the steps involved in creating a mural? Number these steps in order from 1 to 7.

_____ Fill in the outline with color and add details.

_____ Draw sketches of the mural on paper.

_____ Draw an outline of the mural on the wall.

_____ Gather brushes, paint, and other necessary materials.

_____ Paint the wall with primer or white paint.

_____ Choose a subject or theme.

_____ Scrape and wash the wall.

Now Presenting...

Beauty and the Beast

A kind and beautiful young woman releases a man from the spell that has turned him into a hideous beast.

Setting the Stage

Background

Tell students that this play is based on a story that is at least 300 years old, and perhaps much older than that. In the eighteenth century, fairy tales were published and used by tutors to teach their pupils important moral lessons. These stories often involved princes and princesses or other royalty. Enchantment and romance were also important elements. Ask students to share anything they already know about *Beauty and the Beast* or any other fairy tale that they know.

Staging

On the board or on butcher paper, students may draw a busy seaport, a small cottage in the woods, and a fabulous castle, all connected by a country road. Have readers sit in front of the different scenes as appropriate during the reading.

Encore

Students may wish to compare this script to other versions of this fairy tale. You might view the film version by Disney, for example, and ask students to compare it to a print version, such as Della Rowland's *Beauty and the Beast.*

Vocabulary

Introduce and discuss the following words before reading the script:

creditor: a person who gives someone credit, or to whom money is owed

merchant: a person whose business is the buying and selling of goods

sumptuous: lavish; involving great expense

trellis: a structure, usually of thin strips of woods, used to train climbing plants

vain: conceited

widower: a man whose wife has died

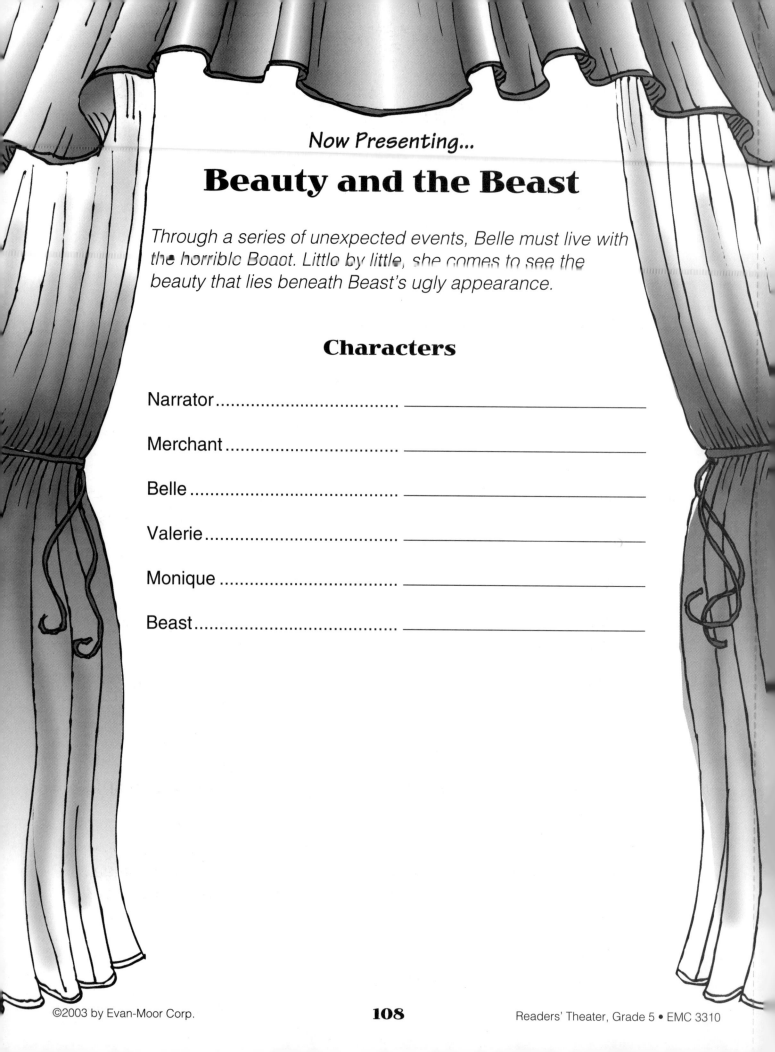

Now Presenting...

Beauty and the Beast

Through a series of unexpected events, Belle must live with the horrible Beast. Little by little, she comes to see the beauty that lies beneath Beast's ugly appearance.

Characters

Narrator.................................... _____

Merchant.................................. _____

Belle .... _____

Valerie..................................... _____

Monique .... _____

Beast.. _____

Beauty and the Beast

································· **Characters** ·························

Narrator	Valerie
Merchant	Monique
Belle	Beast

··

Narrator: A long, long time ago in a city by the sea, there lived a wealthy merchant and his three daughters. A widower for many years, the merchant loved his daughters dearly and spared no expense on their behalf. Of course, they had grown very used to their lifestyle of comfort. Sadly, their fortune collapsed one chilly winter day.

Merchant: My dearest daughters, we are ruined. Three of my ships have been lost at sea. Now we must sell off everything of value that we own in order to pay my creditors.

Belle: But where will we go, Father?

Merchant: Your mother had a small house in the country. We shall have to move there.

Valerie: In the country? You can't be serious, Father. Do you expect us to marry farmers?

Monique: This is perfectly dreadful!

Merchant: We'll have to make the best of it. Now pack up all of your belongings. We must leave tomorrow.

Narrator: The next day, the family traveled by carriage to the mountains on the other side of the river. They would have to grow their own vegetables and mend their own clothes from now on. Valerie and Monique were none too happy about it.

Valerie: We've only been here for a week and already I have blisters on my fingers. This isn't the life for me, I can tell you.

Monique: Believe me, I'm getting married the first chance I get. My Prince Charming will take me away from all this drudgery.

Belle: In the meantime, we should try to make this as easy as possible on Father. This is hard for him too.

Narrator: A month later, word came to the merchant that one of his ships had been found. He rushed to tell his daughters.

Merchant: I should go back to the city at once to reclaim some of our lost fortune.

Monique: We're rich again! I can hardly wait to move back to the city! You'll have to buy us some suitable dresses while you're there.

Valerie: And some hats and jewelry too, since we had to sell it all.

Merchant: What about you, Belle? What can I get you?

Belle: A rose, Father. That's all I want.

Merchant: Then I shall bring you the finest rose I can find.

Narrator: The merchant rode his horse to the seaport as fast he could. He found out that his property had been seized to pay for his debts. Now he had to go back to his cottage in the woods, with even less money than before. On the way, there was a severe snowstorm. Through the snowfall, he saw a dim light in the distance. He followed the light and, to his astonishment, found himself before a fabulous castle.

Merchant: How very strange. The courtyards are all lit up, but there are no servants around. It must be time for supper, though, because I can smell roasted meat and herbs. Surely the master won't mind if I join him, under the circumstances.

Narrator: The merchant let himself in through the front door. A sumptuous meal was set on the table, as if waiting for him. He helped himself to one of the finest meals he had ever eaten. Afterward, he began to explore the castle.

Merchant: In all my travels, I've never seen such exquisite taste. Surely a kind and gentle soul lives here. Everything has been arranged with loving care. I do wish I could meet the master so I could thank him for his kindness.

Narrator: The merchant wandered down a hallway until he came to an open door. Inside, he saw a bed with the covers turned down. Utterly exhausted, he crawled in and immediately fell asleep. In the morning, he mounted his horse and prepared to leave. Near the castle gate, he passed a trellis with beautiful red roses, and he thought of Belle.

Merchant: My poor daughters will be so disappointed in me, but at least Belle can have the rose she wanted.

Narrator: As the merchant picked the rose, a frightening beast sprang forward. The merchant was startled out of his wits, for he had never seen a creature quite like this. It was dressed in the finest suit, but had the face of a wild and deformed animal.

Beast: You ungrateful man! I saved your life, and you repay me by stealing my roses! These flowers mean more to me than anything. For this you shall die.

Merchant: Please, sire. Have mercy. It is true you have been very generous to me. I picked the flower for my daughter, not for myself.

Beast: I will spare your life on one condition. Bring your daughter here. Then you will know what it is like to live without beauty. If you fail to bring her here, you will pay the ultimate price.

Narrator: With a heavy heart, the merchant returned to his humble cottage. His daughters were frantic upon hearing his story.

Valerie: Will the tragedies never end?

Monique: This is all your fault, Belle! If only you hadn't asked for a rose, none of this would have happened.

Belle: Dear Father, please let me go to the castle as the beast demands. After all you've done for us, it's the least I can do for you.

Merchant: No, Belle. I will let no harm come to my daughters.

Narrator: That evening, Belle snuck outside. She had no idea how she would get to the castle, yet she found a white steed waiting for her. She mounted it, and it whisked her to the castle at lightning speed. As she entered, Belle marveled at all she saw. Suddenly, the beast appeared before her.

Beast: May I invite you to dine?

Belle: Thank you, but I haven't an appetite.

Beast: Is it because I'm so hideous to look at?

Belle: I will not lie to you, Beast. You have spared my father's life. The least I can do is be honest with you. It is true you frighten me. Please give me time to get used to my new situation.

Beast: Thank you, Belle. If you will permit me, I will meet you again tomorrow evening. Make yourself at home, for everything in the castle is yours.

Narrator: Belle passed the next day in the garden, alone. That evening, she seated herself at the dining table. Beast appeared as before, and they chatted together while they ate. Belle almost forgot how frightening Beast was to look at.

Beast: Do you think you could be happy here? Is there anything you want?

Belle: If I could have my own rose garden, that would give me great pleasure. Flowers are the most precious thing in the world to me.

Beast: You shall have whatever you want. Belle, would you ever consent to be my wife?

Belle: No, Beast. That can never happen. I swore to you that I would always tell the truth. I cannot marry you, because I do not love you.

Narrator: And so the days passed. Every evening, Beast joined Belle for dinner. They drank, ate, laughed, and talked. Now and again, Beast asked Belle if she would marry him. She regretfully declined his offer each time. One night, she had a dream that her father was ill, and she begged Beast to let her go. She promised that she would return the next day, and he agreed. Once again, the white steed whisked her home.

Belle: I had a dream you were ill, Father. Are you all right?

Merchant: Ever since Valerie and Monique married and moved away, it's been more difficult for me to manage. But tell me: What is your life like? What is it like to live with that beast? Does he frighten you?

Belle: It's not so bad, Father. I've actually become fond of him. He treats me very well.

Merchant: I can't stand the thought of never seeing you, Belle. Please stay here just one more night.

Belle: I told Beast I would return today, but I will stay one more night, Father, if it makes you feel better.

Narrator: The next day, Belle rushed back to the castle as quickly as she could. She knew she would find Beast in his rose garden. There he was, dying of a broken heart, for he thought Belle had decided not to come back. Even his precious roses had withered and died.

Belle: Here I am, Beast. Please don't leave me. Until this moment I felt only friendship for you. Now I know that I love you. Please stay with me and let me be your wife.

Narrator: Before Belle's very eyes, the roses bloomed once again, and Beast was transformed into a handsome young man.

Belle: Where is my Beast? What have you done with him?

Beast: I am Beast, Belle. I was once very vain. I judged people by their appearances. For this I was changed into a hideous monster. With your kindness, you have brought beauty back into my heart.

Narrator: Belle and her beloved lived together for the rest of their lives. Although their youth and their good looks faded over time, their love for each other was always fresh and forever young.

Name _____

Story Map

Complete the story map to summarize the plot of the story.

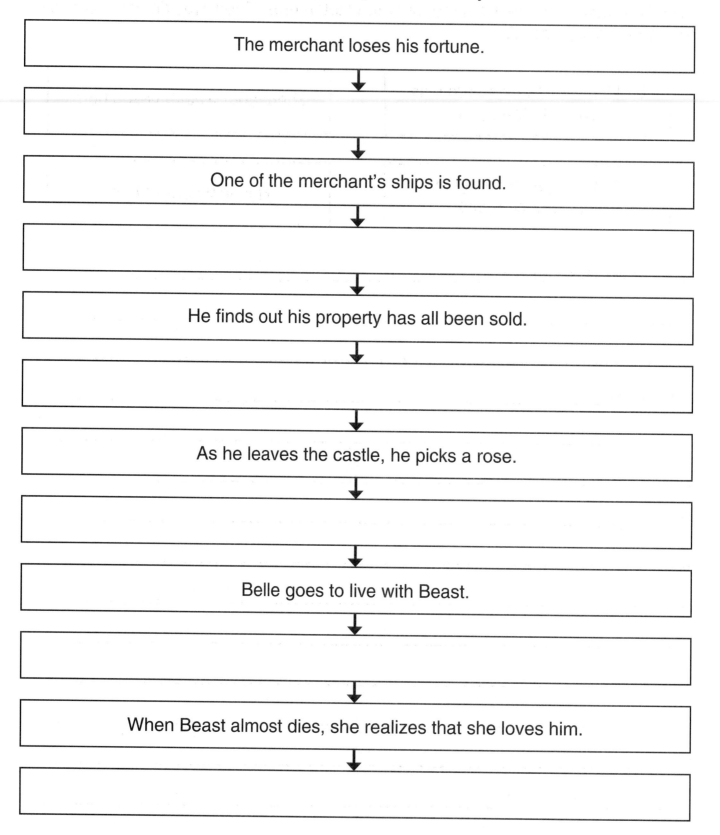

The merchant loses his fortune.

↓

↓

One of the merchant's ships is found.

↓

↓

He finds out his property has all been sold.

↓

↓

As he leaves the castle, he picks a rose.

↓

↓

Belle goes to live with Beast.

↓

↓

When Beast almost dies, she realizes that she loves him.

↓

   Readers' Theater, Grade 5 • EMC 3310

Name _____

The Moral of the Story

Most fairy tales have a moral, or lesson. In your opinion, what is the moral of *Beauty and the Beast*? Choose from the following statements. Then provide your reasons for choosing that moral.

Be kind to those who are less fortunate than you.	Share your wealth with others.
Don't judge someone by appearance alone.	Respect your elders.

Moral of the Story: _____

_____

_____

Reason: _____

_____

_____

_____

_____

_____

_____

_____

_____

Now Presenting...

The Runaways

In the late 1700s, a family of runaway slaves seeks shelter in the home of a white family in the colony of Rhode Island. The family must decide whether to risk the wrath of their pro-slavery neighbors by doing what they know is right and helping the runaways.

Setting the Stage

Background

Review with students some of the major events related to the slave era and the American Revolutionary War. Throughout the eighteenth century, the thirteen colonies expanded at a rapid rate and prospered, largely because of the free labor they extracted from slaves. This was particularly true of the southern colonies, where slavery was critical to profit. As their wealth increased, colonists began to resent British rule. Throughout most of the century, British control had been lax, but Britain became more concerned with gaining tighter control of the colonies in the latter half of the century. In 1765 Britain decided to impose the Stamp Act, which was the first form of direct taxation on the colonies. Outraged colonists protested British taxation at the Boston Tea Party of 1773, and this led to an all-out military conflict. When war broke out, many slaves took advantage of the disruption and fled the plantations where they had been enslaved. This play is a fictional account of one such family.

Staging

You may draw on the board a simple farmhouse connected to a patch of woods by a dirt path. Have readers stand in front of different parts of the scene as appropriate while reading their lines.

Encore

Students may want to learn more about slavery in the context of the American Revolution after reading this play. In recent years, there has been a tremendous amount of very good research that is now available on the Internet. Students can do a search using the key words *slavery* and *American Revolution*.

Vocabulary

Introduce and discuss the following words before reading the script:

flapjacks: pancakes

hands: workers

plantation: a large farm

redcoats: British soldiers

revolutionaries: people involved in an armed struggle against a government

suspicious: showing or expressing doubt

wager: to bet

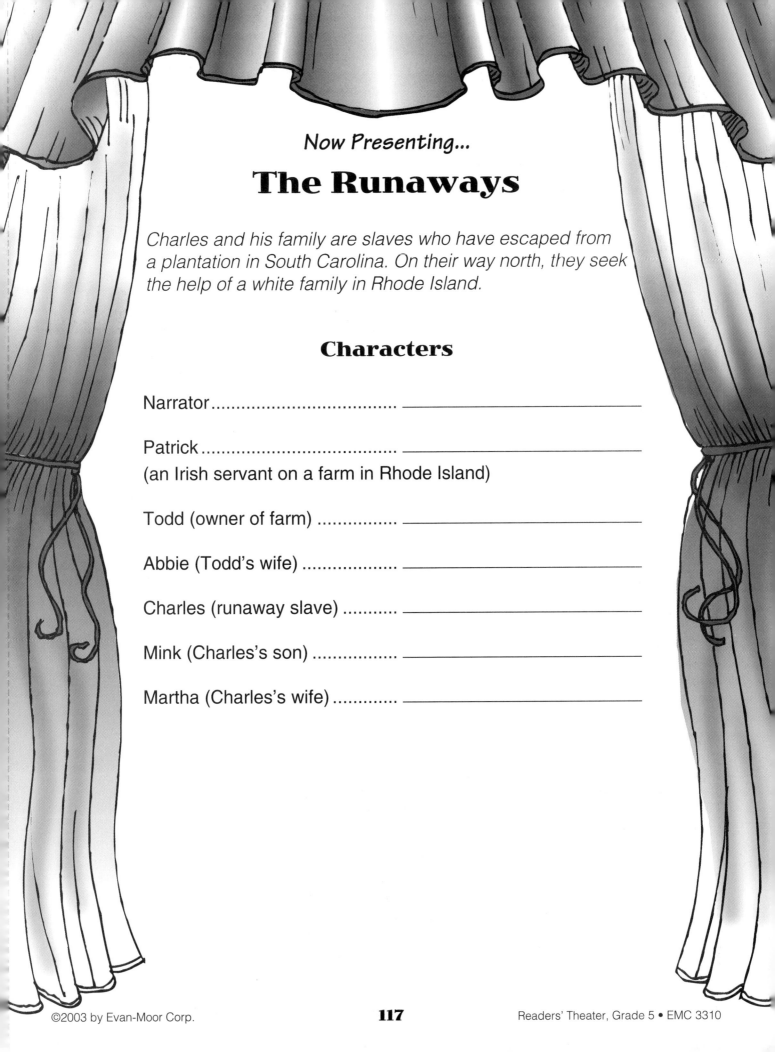

Now Presenting...

The Runaways

Charles and his family are slaves who have escaped from a plantation in South Carolina. On their way north, they seek the help of a white family in Rhode Island.

Characters

Narrator .... _____

Patrick .... _____
(an Irish servant on a farm in Rhode Island)

Todd (owner of farm) .... _____

Abbie (Todd's wife) .... _____

Charles (runaway slave) .... _____

Mink (Charles's son) .... _____

Martha (Charles's wife) .... _____

The Runaways

········· **Characters** ·········

Narrator Charles
Patrick Martha
Todd Mink
Abbie

Narrator: In the late 1700s, the thirteen colonies were engaged in a war with Britain to gain their independence. Many slaves took advantage of the confusion caused by the war to escape. Charles Johnson was one example. In the face of great danger, he stole away with his wife, Martha, and his son, Mink. After many days and nights on the run, they stop to rest near a farm in Rhode Island. There they are spotted by a servant on the farm.

Patrick: *(entering house breathlessly)* Master! Missus! Look out yonder by the edge of the woods!

Abbie: *(peering out window)* Look at that! There's three of 'em. They must be a family, by the looks of it.

Patrick: They sure look tired and scared.

Todd: How long have they been there?

Patrick: I don't know, but they were there when I went out to fetch the water. I'll wager they spent the night right there in the woods.

Todd: Did anybody else see them?

Patrick: Well, not that I know.

Todd: Then don't say a word, not even to the horse. You hear me?

Patrick: Yes, Master.

Todd: Now go get some wood.

Patrick: Right away. *(leaves)*

Todd: Martha, you know what this is about.

Abbie: I sure do. They're on the run. I'll bet they're trying to get away from some horrible place down south where they had to suffer who knows what. Look at the young one. He can't be much older than 12, if he's a day. I can hear his stomach growl all the way from here. I've a mind to cook 'em all some flapjacks and bacon.

Todd: Don't be gettin' involved, Abbie. We've talked about this a hundred times.

Abbie: It's the least we can do, Todd. I'm not saying let's take 'em in and give 'em room and board. But can't we at least let 'em rest here for a while?

Todd: It's asking for trouble, and you know it. In case you forgot, there's plenty of slave owners 'round these parts. Imagine what would happen to us if they heard about this.

Abbie: They've all got the war on their minds. Besides, slavery is just wrong. I know you feel the same way about it that I do.

Todd: That doesn't mean we have to start our own war. Isn't one enough? You want to fight the redcoats and the slave owners both?

Abbie: You can turn me in if you want, but I'm helpin' those people!

Patrick: *(entering)* Here's the wood, Master.

Abbie: Patrick, take this pitcher of lemon water out to those people and give 'em a drink. Then ask 'em to come up into the house.

Patrick: Am I hearing right, Master?

Todd: Do as she says, Patrick.

Narrator: Patrick took the pitcher and some cups down into the woods. He stood at a distance, watching while the family drank the water and listening as they discussed their situation.

Charles: Those people ain't goin' to help us. It's a trick. They're just goin' to lock us up and turn us in.

Martha: Charles, we got to take a chance. Our boy ain't goin' to last much longer. He needs somethin' to eat. You can't expect a boy to live on berries and leaves. It's been five days since we've had real food.

Charles: All right then, you stay here with Mink. I'll go talk to them first. If you hear me holler, then you take off runnin' and don't look back. Mink, you take care of your mama, all right?

Mink: Yes, Papa. We'll stay right here till you come back.

Narrator: Charles and Patrick walked up to the house together. On the way, Charles tried to find out all he could from Patrick.

Charles: You work here on the farm?

Patrick: I sure do.

Charles: By yourself? Where's all the slaves?

Patrick: This farm ain't so big that we need more hands. It's just me and the master and missus. There's only apple orchards and a few animals. When harvest time comes, we hire servants from the farm down a ways.

Charles: You mean you pay people to work for you? You don't make 'em work for free?

Patrick: That's right. Master and Missus don't believe in that. I myself was a servant down in Georgia. It was as close to bein' a slave as I ever want to come. Mr. Smith had me workin' from dawn till night. All I ever got for it was a sore back. When Mr. Smith said I could have my freedom after seven years, I was more than happy to say good-bye!

Narrator: Todd and Abbie were waiting for Patrick and Charles on the front porch. Charles took off his hat and introduced himself.

Charles: Afternoon, mister and missus. I'm mighty grateful for the water. My name's Charles Johnson. Over there's my wife and son.

Todd: Welcome, Charles. You're safe with us. We don't mean you any harm.

Charles: Those sure are soothin' words.

Todd: Now why don't you tell us what brings you 'round here?

Charles: We ran away from a plantation down in South Carolina. That's the long and short of it. I figured we'd come up north, maybe all the way to Boston. Hopefully, I'll have my chance to help the cause.

Abbie: You mean you're goin' to fight with the Patriots against the British?

Charles: That's my intention. I hear the revolutionaries talkin' about the rights of all men to be free, and that sounds mighty good to me. Maybe, when we get our independence from England, we can *all* be free.

Abbie: I do hope so, Charles. Now why don't you bring your missus and boy up here? We were just about to have breakfast.

Charles: Martha! Mink! Come on up!

Martha and Mink: We're comin'!

Narrator: Charles and his family spent the whole day in the house because they were afraid somebody might see them. The next day, they got up at dawn and prepared to leave. Todd, Abbie, and Patrick all came out to say good-bye.

Abbie: Be careful. And stay away from the road.

Todd: You should be able to get to Massachusetts in less than a week, if you keep walkin'. Then you'll be free.

Martha: Thank you for everything, Mister Todd and Miss Abbie. I think you saved our lives.

Abbie: We're glad to do what we can.

Mink: Thanks for the new shirt, Miss Abbie. And the flapjacks too! I'll be thinkin' about those flapjacks all the way to Boston.

Abbie: You're quite welcome, Mink. Now, you take this bundle of food for your journey.

Charles: I can't tell you how thankful we are!

Todd: You don't have to. Just keep goin'. Freedom's waitin' up the road. *(exit Charles, Martha, and Mink)*

Patrick: I wonder if we'll ever hear from them again?

Abbie: Who knows? Lots of changes are comin'. One day, these thirteen colonies might just form one nation. If so, we can make laws that are just and abide by them.

Todd: Then people might be free to come and go as they please, no matter their color.

Patrick: I hope you're right, Mister and Missus. I hope you're right.

What Would You Do?

Todd and Abbie had to decide whether they should help a family of runaway slaves. What would you do if you were faced with their decision? Write a paragraph explaining what you would do. Be sure to give at least three reasons to support your decision.

_____

_____

_____

_____

_____

_____

_____

_____

_____

_____

_____

_____

_____

_____

Name _____

The Road to Freedom

Study the map. Then complete the sentences using information from the map.

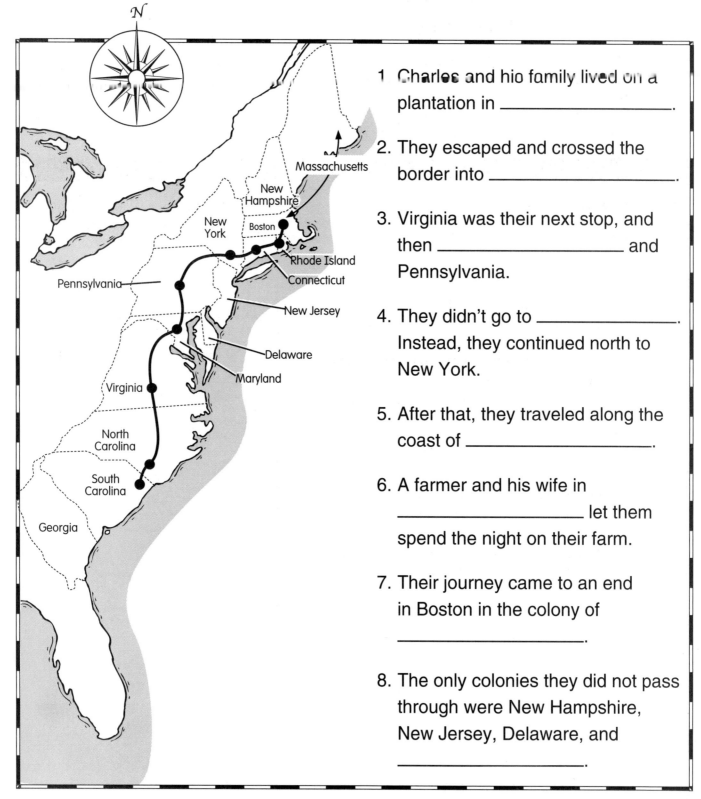

1. Charles and his family lived on a plantation in _____.

2. They escaped and crossed the border into _____.

3. Virginia was their next stop, and then _____ and Pennsylvania.

4. They didn't go to _____. Instead, they continued north to New York.

5. After that, they traveled along the coast of _____.

6. A farmer and his wife in _____ let them spend the night on their farm.

7. Their journey came to an end in Boston in the colony of _____.

8. The only colonies they did not pass through were New Hampshire, New Jersey, Delaware, and _____.

Now Presenting...

Princess Ka`iulani of Hawai`i

Princess Ka`iulani of Hawai`i lived at a time of radical change. She witnessed Hawai`i's overthrow by American businessmen and its annexation to the United States. Although she never actually ruled, she is remembered as "the last princess of Hawai`i."

Setting the Stage

Background

Display a map of the United States and point out Hawai`i to students. Explain that the state of Hawai`i is actually a chain of 132 islands. There are eight main islands in the southeastern end of the chain. The island called Hawai`i is the largest one and gives its name to the state. Throughout most of the 1800s, Hawai`i was ruled by a monarchy. The monarchy was overthrown by U.S. Marines in 1893, however, and the islands were annexed in 1898. This play presents several vignettes from the life of Princess Ka`iulani, who was heir to the throne at the time of the U.S. takeover.

Encore

Students may enjoy reading *The Last Princess: The Story of Princess Ka`iulani of Hawai`i,* a picture book by Fay Stanley. For a more detailed biography, you may refer students to *Princess Ka`iulani: Hope of a Nation, Heart of a People* by Sharon Linnéa.

Vocabulary

Introduce and discuss the following words before reading the script:

annex: to make a territory, state, or country part of another country

monarch: the single ruler of a nation; a king or queen

monarchy: rule of a nation by a king or queen

rational: logical or sensible

vested: to be given an absolute, total right

Now Presenting

Princess Ka`iulani
of Hawai`i

*Ka`iulani is remembered as "the last princess of Hawai`i."
She tried her best to represent the wishes of her people and
prevent the annexation of her country to the United States.*

Characters

Narrator 1 .... _____

Narrator 2 .... _____

Princess Ka`iulani .... _____

Princess Likelike .... _____
(Princess Ka`iulani's mother)

Princess Ka`iulani's Guardian... _____

President Cleveland .... _____

Princess Ka`iulani of Hawai`i

································· **Characters** ·····························

Narrator 1   Princess Likelike
Narrator 2   Princess Ka`iulani's Guardian
Princess Ka`iulani   President Cleveland

··

Narrator 1: In the 1800s Hawai`i was a nation ruled by monarchs. King Kalakaua and Queen Kapi`olani were vested with power for life. They had no children of their own, and so the crown was to pass to a niece or nephew of the king.

Narrator 2: All of Hawai`i was overjoyed when at last a baby girl was born to Princess Likelike, the king's sister, on October 16, 1875. The child's name was Ka`iulani, which means "the royal sacred one." Princess Ka`iulani's childhood was a happy one. She had peacocks and a pony as pets, and she could go swimming at the beach anytime she liked.

Narrator 1: At the young age of 11 years, however, she would experience a very deep loss. Her mother was gravely ill. When she called for her daughter, Princess Ka`iulani knew it might be the last time she saw her beloved mother.

Likelike: I'm very ill, Ka`iulani, but I have something important to tell you.

Ka`iulani: Please try to save your strength, Mama.

Likelike: I have seen your future plain and clear, and I want to tell you what I saw. It is this: You will go away for a very long time. You will never marry. And you will never be queen.

Ka`iulani: Mama, please. I don't want to know. I just want you to get better.

Likelike: Go now. But remember what I said.

Narrator 1: Ka`iulani wept as she was led from the room. Her mother's words hung in the air. They had the certainty of a person on the brink of death. Her mother did indeed pass away that very afternoon. Ka`iulani was now second in line to the throne, after her Aunt Lili`uokalani.

Narrator 2: Several years later, at the age of 14, Ka`iulani was sent to a boarding school in England. The first part of her mother's prediction had come true. As she stood on the steamship, she shared her thoughts about her past and future with her guardian.

Ka`iulani: I shall never completely recover from my mother's death. Now my chief aim in life is to serve my people in whatever way I can.

Guardian: And that is exactly why you are going to London. There you will receive the best education available at this time. As a queen, you will need to speak several different languages. You will have to entertain heads of state and make decisions of the utmost importance. It won't be an easy life. I hope you're prepared.

Ka`iulani: But don't you remember my mother's words? She said I would never be queen. Why would she say such a thing?

Guardian: Ka`iulani, people say all sorts of things when they are as ill as your mother was. They are not completely rational. I know you have deep respect for your mother's last words, but try to put them in the proper context.

Ka`iulani: I will. I will try my best.

Narrator 2: The trip was very difficult for Ka`iulani, because she had never traveled before, and now she had to cross two oceans and a continent. After she settled down, Ka`iulani enjoyed her years at the boarding school in London. She studied French, German, English, history, music, and the social graces necessary for a queen. She attended parties and made many acquaintances.

Narrator 1: While she was in England, important changes were taking place in Hawai`i. One day, her guardian brought her news of these events.

Guardian: Princess Ka`iulani, may I speak with you in private?

Ka`iulani: What is it?

Guardian: Tell me, what have you heard about Hawai`i these last few months?

**Ka`iulani:** I know that the situation has gone from bad to worse. Foreigners, mostly Americans, have grown rich with their sugarcane plantations. They've bought up all the land. Now they have a stake in the future of Hawai`i, and because of that they want to have some say in the course of things.

Guardian: Unfortunately, they've become impatient and resorted to force. The businessmen you speak of have used their wealth and power to force King Kalakaua to accept a new constitution. The new constitution has weakened the monarchy. Worse, the businessmen want to annex Hawai`i.

Ka`iulani: You mean they want to make it part of the United States?

Guardian: Exactly.

Ka`iulani: What can I do?

Guardian: Nothing for the moment, I'm afraid. We'll just have to wait—and hope.

Narrator 1: Events started unfolding quickly thereafter. In 1891 King Kalakaua died of an unknown illness. His wife, and Ka`iulani's aunt, Lili`uokalani, became queen. That made Ka`iulani next in line for the throne.

Narrator 2: Aunt Lili`u, as Ka`iulani called her, tried to resist the foreign takeover. The American business interests felt threatened by her and decided to take action. Events came to a climax on January 16, 1893. News traveled very slowly in those days. Ka`iulani did not hear of the American invasion until several weeks later. Once again, it was her guardian who informed her of the bad news.

Guardian: Prepare yourself for the worst, Ka`iulani. American Marines have marched into Honolulu and, and—they overthrew Queen Lili`uokalani!

Ka`iulani: *(gasping)* You mean . . .?

Guardian: *(sighing)* Yes, the monarchy has come to an end.

**Ka`iulani:** I am no longer the crown princess of Hawai`i! My people are no longer rulers of their own destiny.

Guardian: Perhaps there is something you could do after all, Ka`iulani, if only as a last resort.

Ka`iulani: What is that?

Guardian: Well, the United States has just elected a new president. You might be able to reason with him. This is an unlawful takeover of a sovereign nation. Surely the president will want to restore law.

Narrator 1: Ka`iulani decided to go to Washington to personally speak to the new president, Grover Cleveland. Even though she was just 17 years old, she hoped there was *something* she could say or do to help her people.

**Ka`iulani:** President Cleveland, I come before you on behalf of my people. I am just a student, not a politician. Nevertheless, I implore you to consider our plight. Queen Lili`uokalani cannot come before you because she is a prisoner in her very own home!

Cleveland: Of course, I've talked to the U.S. businesses involved in the matter. Their argument is that they've developed Hawai`i, and so they have a right to political representation. Isn't that fair?

Ka`iulani: It's certainly *not* fair that Hawaiians are treated as foreigners in their own country. Many Hawaiians do not even have the right to vote.

Cleveland: That is distressing. I am very impressed that a person of your age cares so deeply about the future of her people.

**Ka`iulani:** The people of Hawai`i are suffering, Mr. President. Their suffering has given me strength to come all this way to ask you to help us.

Cleveland: I assure you that justice *will* be done, Princess Ka`iulani. I've decided that Hawai`i will *not* be annexed—for the time being. Meanwhile, I will send a representative to Hawai`i to investigate the true state of affairs.

Ka`iulani: Mr. President, I'm overjoyed at this news. Thank you ever so much for your generosity and compassion.

Narrator 2: The meeting was a success. Princess Ka`iulani was front-page news across the country. Before she went back to England, Ka`iulani made a statement to the press.

Ka`iulani: Before I leave the land, I want to thank all whose kindnesses have made my visit such a happy one. Not only the hundreds of hands I have clasped or the kind smiles I have seen, but the written words of sympathy that have been sent to me from so many homes, have made me feel that whatever happens to me I shall never be a stranger to you again. It was to all the American people I spoke, and they heard me as I knew they would.

Narrator 1: Sadly, Princess Ka`iulani's efforts were in vain. Princess Ka`iulani returned to her homeland on November 9, 1897. Hawai`i was annexed by the United States on August 12, 1898. She tried her best to comfort her fellow countrymen, but her heart was broken, and she died on March 6, 1899. Her death was very sudden and came as a shock to her fellow Hawaiians. Thousands of people marched in a procession in her honor.

Narrator 2: Her mother's prediction had come true after all. Princess Ka`iulani had traveled very far, had never married, and never became queen. Still, she is a source of pride. Hawaiians admire her purity and innocence. Princess Ka`iulani showed remarkable strength for a person of her age.

The Life of Princess Ka`iulani

Fill in the writing lines below to tell important events from Princess Ka`iulani's life. Write about her early years in Hawai`i and her time in England and Washington, D.C. Conclude by writing about her return to her homeland.

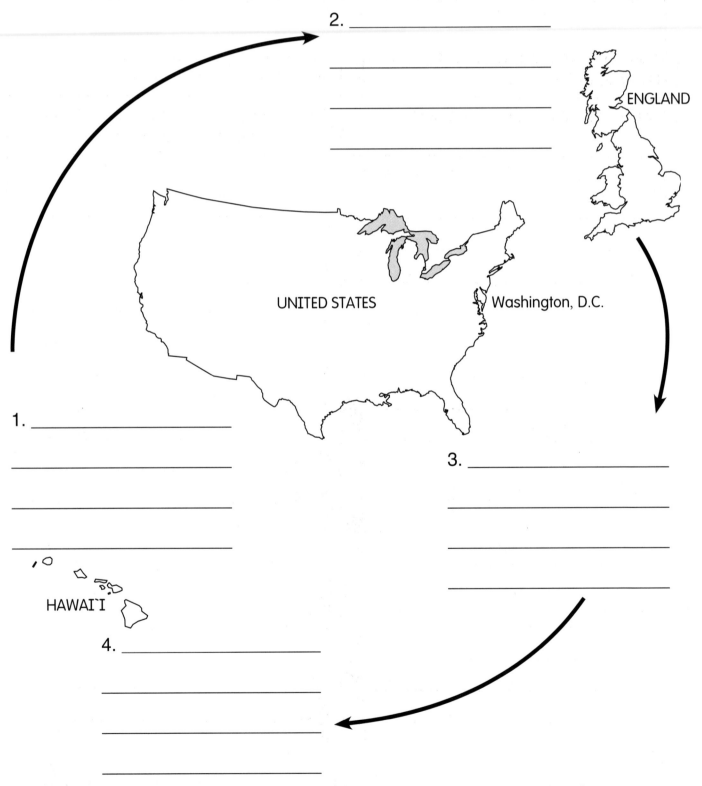

2. _____

_____

_____

_____

ENGLAND

UNITED STATES   Washington, D.C.

1. _____

_____

_____

3. _____

_____

_____

HAWAI`I

4. _____

_____

_____

Name _____

A Brief History of Hawai`i

Make a time line using the dates and events in the table.

1900–The United States establishes the Territory of Hawai`i.	**1872**–King Kalakaua takes the throne.
1894–The United States recognizes the Republic of Hawai`i.	**1896**–The first Hawaiian governor, John Waihee, takes office.
1898–The United States annexes Hawai`i.	**1893**–Queen Lili`uokalani is overthrown by American business interests.
1891–Queen Lili`uokalani succeeds King Kalakaua.	**1959**–Hawai`i becomes the 50th American state.

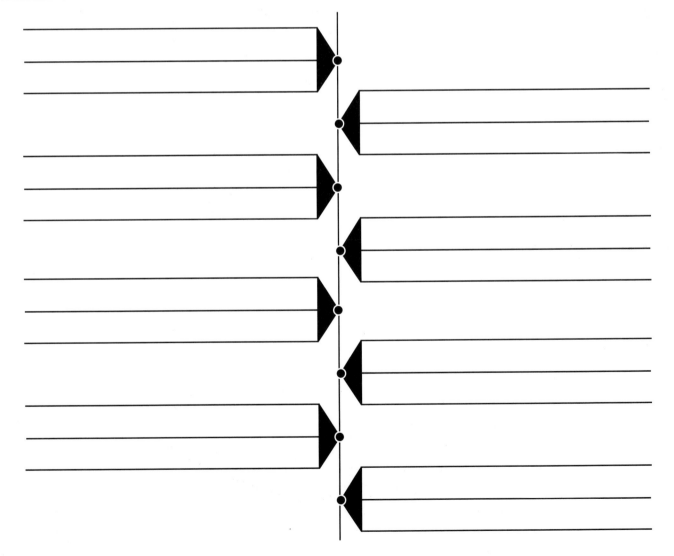

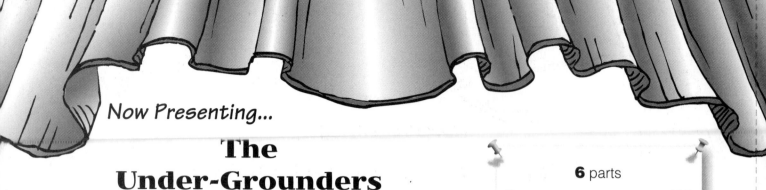

Now Presenting...

The Under-Grounders

In this futuristic fantasy, a young boy escapes from an underground dome to see if there is still life on the surface of Earth.

Setting the Stage

Background

Lead a discussion about films and books that present different visions of the future. Help students to identify common themes throughout these works. In many stories about the future, Earth is barely habitable and humans are forced to live under harsh conditions, often in a kind of police-state. Tell students that the play they are about to read is set in a future in which humans have sealed themselves up in huge underground domes due to massive global warming. With students, imagine what such a future might be like. Ask: How would people produce food and obtain water? How would they generate electricity and get rid of waste? This discussion will help to set the stage for the futuristic atmosphere of the play.

Staging

Dim the lights and, if possible, have students read by flashlight to reproduce an underground atmosphere.

Encore

View and read other futuristic works with students such as *2001: A Space Odyssey, Planet of the Apes,* and *The Time Machine.* Encourage students to create outlines for their own science fiction stories, which they may develop into scripts in small groups.

Vocabulary

Introduce and discuss the following words before reading the script:

ozone: a layer of the atmosphere that surrounds Earth, absorbs radiation from the Sun, and helps to maintain Earth's temperature

perish: to die

reservoir: a place where something is kept in store

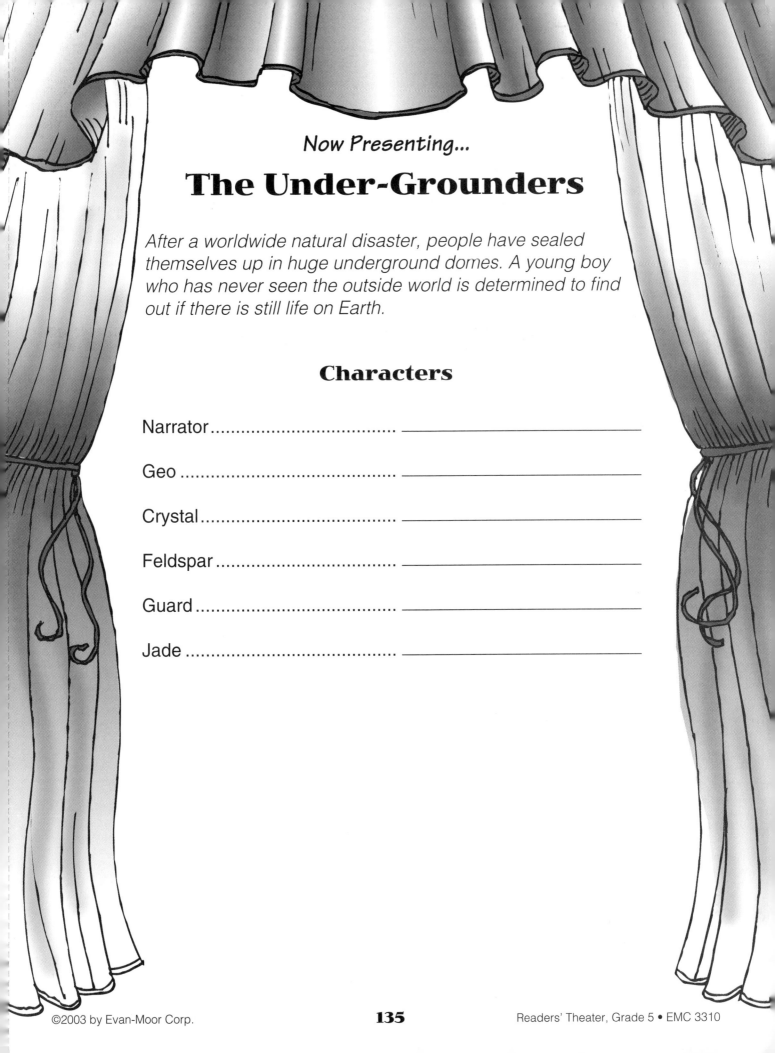

Now Presenting...

The Under-Grounders

After a worldwide natural disaster, people have sealed themselves up in huge underground domes. A young boy who has never seen the outside world is determined to find out if there is still life on Earth.

Characters

Narrator .... ————————————————

Geo .... ————————————————

Crystal....................................... ————————————————

Feldspar .... ————————————————

Guard .... ————————————————

Jade .... ————————————————

Readers' Theater, Grade 5 • EMC 3310

The Under-Grounders

.... **Characters** ....

Narrator	Feldspar
Geo	Guard
Crystal	Jade

Narrator: The year is 2099. In 2060 a number of natural disasters occurred around the world due to global warming. Scientists and technicians began to build underground domes and passageways as temporary shelters. Over time, these "burrows" expanded and grew into dome-like cities. By 2099 the underground cities were sealed. The children who were born and raised underground had never seen the sky or smelled fresh air. Geo and Crystal are two such children.

Geo: Crystal, have you ever tried to imagine what life was like on the surface?

Crystal: Sometimes I do. But it's so hard to imagine, I give up after a while.

Geo: Take the whole idea of day and night, for example. It's so weird. Everybody went to bed at night, when the Sun was down, and got up in the morning, when the Sun was up. It's funny that most people all went to sleep at about the same time. It must have been quiet at night.

Crystal: It's certainly different now. There's not enough space to have everybody up and walking around all at the same time. We all have to sleep in shifts.

Geo: And one day might be different from another day. On some days it was cloudy and windy. On other days it was hot and still. The temperature is always the same down here.

Crystal: It's nice and cool down here. In some ways we might be lucky. I'm not sure I'd like all those extreme changes. Have you ever heard of that thing called "snow"?

Geo: Yeah, but it must have been nice to be on a beach on a sunny day, and to feel the warmth of the sunlight on your face. The thing I'm most curious about is the food. I've heard that fruit grew from plants and trees. Food came right out of the dirt!

Crystal: Honestly, Geo. You should just stop thinking about it. What good is it? I don't like to torture myself thinking about things I'll never be able to experience.

Geo: But maybe there are still plants and trees and sunny days and starry nights. Maybe we *will* be able to go back up to the surface one day.

Crystal: I'm afraid not, Geo. Everything was scorched by the radiation of the Sun. The ozone layer was totally depleted, and Earth was unprotected. If you were to go back to the surface—assuming there was a way, which there isn't—you would find nothing but ashes and dust.

Geo: But surely there must be *somebody* who has actually been there. I'd like to at least *hear* about it.

Crystal: Do you know the old one at the edge of the dome?

Geo: The long-hair?

Crystal: That's the one. His name is Feldspar. I heard that he was one of the last people to come down. You could go talk to him about it. And if you do, keep it to yourself. I'm tired of hearing about the surface.

Narrator: Geo went to talk to Feldspar. The old man was eager to share his memories of life on the surface. They sat and talked together while sharing food wafers.

Geo: Thanks, old man.

Feldspar: For the food wafers? You're quite welcome. Back on the surface, food had *real* texture. It wasn't all just wafers. Watermelon, for example. It was cold and juicy. The inside was red with rows of black seeds. Delicious!

Geo: Is it true that food came right out of the dirt?

Feldspar: In a way of speaking, yes. Plants grew from the ground, and the plants bore fruit.

Geo: What did a plant look like?

Feldspar: There were different kinds. Some were smaller than your hand, but other plants called trees were taller than the central dome.

Geo: Wow!

Feldspar: I still have a flower that I grabbed right before I came underground. I've been saving it all these years between two metal info-discs. Here, let me show you.

Narrator: Feldspar pulled two metal plates from a shelf built into a rocky ledge. He carefully laid them on a stone table and lifted the top plate. A flattened marigold lay on the bottom plate, faded and dry, but still golden. In his excitement, Geo tried to lift the flower, but it crumbled into dust.

Geo: Feldspar, I'm sorry! I didn't mean to ruin it!

Feldspar: It's all right, Geo. Things aren't meant to last forever. I'm glad I got to share it with you.

Geo: Feldspar, I want to go to the surface myself. I want to smell flowers and feel the wind.

Feldspar: That would be very dangerous, Geo. I wouldn't recommend it.

Geo: But there is a way, right?

Feldspar: Yes, there is. But don't ask me about it.

Geo: Feldspar, I *have* to know! You've just *got* to tell me. Please!

Feldspar: There's a secret tunnel, if you must know. Hardly anybody else knows about it. A few people have left by that tunnel over the years, but none of them have come back. They probably didn't survive.

Geo: Or maybe they did, and they didn't want to come back.

Feldspar: I would try it myself, but I'm too old now.

Geo: Then let me try for you.

Feldspar: You really mean it, don't you?

Geo: I've never been more serious.

Feldspar: All right, then. I can tell you have a real desire to know the truth. Go to the reservoir. It's fed by an underground stream. Jump in at the edge by the rock wall, and swim through the underwater tunnel. You'll come to a cave on the other side. Just keep going in the direction of higher ground. Eventually you'll come to an iron ladder going up a narrow tunnel. That'll take you to the surface.

Narrator: Geo got a waterproof flashlight and wrapped some food wafers in a watertight bag. The only problem was passing a guard at the reservoir.

Guard: Halt! What are you doing here?

Geo: I've come to get some water.

Guard: This isn't an official water source. Get your water from the well at the center of the dome, like everybody else.

Narrator: Geo turned as if he was leaving, but suddenly jumped into the reservoir. The guard tried to stun him with an echo gun, but Geo was already underwater. He swam through the tunnel and came up on the other side. From there, he followed signs that other travelers had written on the cave walls. Eventually, he came to an iron ladder and climbed up to the surface. At first, the light of day was blinding. Through squinted eyes, he thought he could see the figure of a girl his age.

Geo: Who . . . who are you?

Jade: My name is Jade. Welcome to the surface.

Geo: You mean, people are still alive on the surface?

Jade: Plenty. Here, take my hand and come up.

Geo: Thanks. *(picking flower)* Wow! I know what this is. It's called a marigold.

Jade: That's right. There's a whole field of marigolds nearby.

Geo: And those must be trees. I've heard of those too. And clouds! And birds! How can this be true? I thought everything was destroyed by radiation.

Jade: After the ozone disaster, everybody went underground. Most everybody, that is. The poorest of the poor were left to perish on the surface. And many did die. It was horrible. But over time, Earth began to heal itself.

Geo: How is that possible?

Jade: There was no more pollution. Nature at last had a break from the constant outpouring of toxins. Over time, poisons in the ground disintegrated. Smog eventually cleared. The hole in the ozone shrank and shrank until finally the atmosphere was sealed once again. Nature was allowed to thrive.

Geo: How do people live without technology, without science?

Jade: Our lives are much simpler, but we have found it is quite possible to live without all of that. We live in harmony and balance with nature.

Geo: The under-grounders think the surface is just a wasteland. Maybe they should know it's all right to come back up.

Jade: I'm afraid to think of what might happen if they did.

Narrator: Geo looked at Jade, and then at the tunnel leading back to the underground. Clutching the marigold, he made up his mind. He knew in his heart just what he should do.

Name _____

Underground View

What do you think an underground city would look like? Draw a picture below.
Add labels to identify your city's elements.

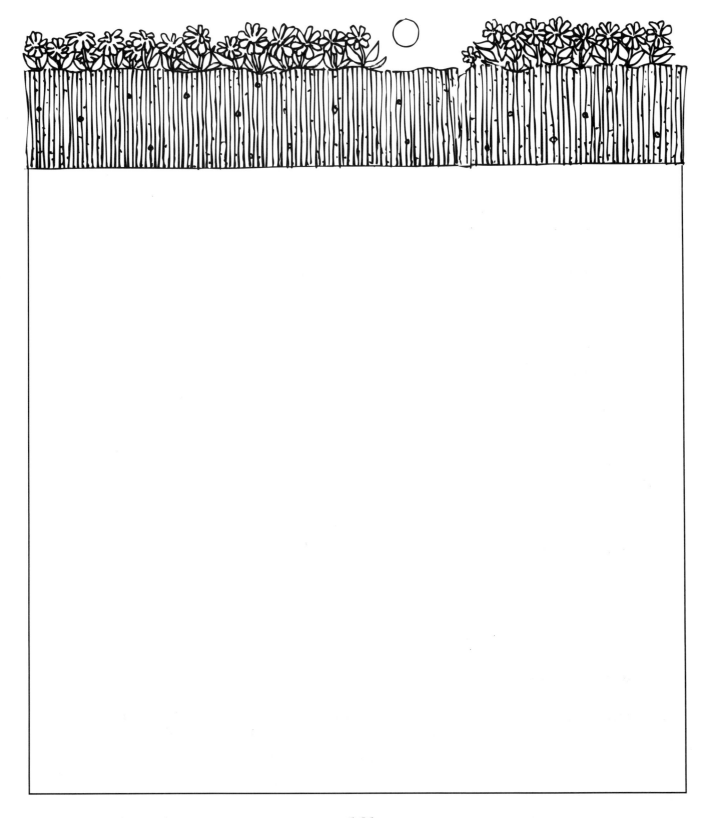

Name _____

Decisions, Decisions

What were the two choices that Geo faced? What are possible consequences of those choices? Fill out the graphic organizer, and then write about the choice you would make, and why.

Geo

Choice: _____

_____

_____

Consequence: _____

_____

_____

_____

Choice: _____

_____

_____

Consequence: _____

_____

_____

_____

Personal Choice: _____

_____

_____

Reason: _____

_____

_____

_____